OECD Reviews of Vocational Education and Training

Engaging Employers in Vocational Education and Training in Brazil

LEARNING FROM INTERNATIONAL PRACTICES

This work is published under the responsibility of the Secretary-General of the OECD. The opinions expressed and arguments employed herein do not necessarily reflect the official views of the Member countries of the OECD.

This document, as well as any data and map included herein, are without prejudice to the status of or sovereignty over any territory, to the delimitation of international frontiers and boundaries and to the name of any territory, city or area.

The statistical data for Israel are supplied by and under the responsibility of the relevant Israeli authorities. The use of such data by the OECD is without prejudice to the status of the Golan Heights, East Jerusalem and Israeli settlements in the West Bank under the terms of international law.

Please cite this publication as:
OECD (2022), *Engaging Employers in Vocational Education and Training in Brazil: Learning from International Practices*, OECD Reviews of Vocational Education and Training, OECD Publishing, Paris, https://doi.org/10.1787/d76a2fe6-en.

ISBN 978-92-64-49915-7 (print)
ISBN 978-92-64-38402-6 (pdf)

OECD Reviews of Vocational Education and Training
ISSN 2077-7728 (print)
ISSN 2077-7736 (online)

Photo credits: Cover © LituFalco/Fotolia.com; Peshkova/Shutterstock.com and Studio Folzer.

Corrigenda to publications may be found on line at: www.oecd.org/about/publishing/corrigenda.htm.
© OECD 2022

The use of this work, whether digital or print, is governed by the Terms and Conditions to be found at https://www.oecd.org/termsandconditions.

Foreword

Strong vocational education and training (VET) smooths the transition of young people into the labour market and facilitates recruitment of skilled workers by employers. Strong VET involves and receives support from social partners, and provides students with an opportunity of continuing in education if they wish to do so.

This OECD report *Engaging Employers in Vocational Education and Training in Brazil: Learning from International Practices,* brings international evidence in areas that are relevant to the reform of VET in Brazil that is now being implemented, and discusses how other countries are addressing related challenges encountered in VET. In Brazil, a minority of students participate in VET, and among those enrolled in VET only a few have an opportunity of training with employers, unlike in many OECD countries. To improve access of young people to VET, Brazil has initiated a series of reforms of its upper secondary VET system. Among other objectives, the reforms aim to expand provision of initial VET by tripling enrolment between 2014-2024.

The report discusses how an expanded and diversified provision of VET can cater to students with different needs, and the importance of supporting schools to deliver VET programmes that correspond with labour market needs and of facilitating access to the VET teacher profession by employees with relevant industry experience. Work-based learning with employers is a key element of high-quality VET, but engaging employers in the provision of training can be challenging. The report discusses measures that can enhance the training capacity of firms, such as training of trainers in companies, and provides examples of how schools and employers can share the responsibility for work-based learning. Strong VET systems involve social partners, including employers and sometimes trade unions, at all levels where decisions about VET are taken, and the report suggests where and how to involve them. Among others, it looks at the role of social partners in planning and undertaking assessments, how this can enhance the quality of assessment, and improve the credibility of certification.

This report was drafted by Małgorzata Kuczera from the OECD Centre for Skills and Simon Field. Marie-Aurélie Elkurd and Jennifer Cannon provided valuable administrative support. Marieke Vandeweyer supported the preparation of this report as manager of the Vocational Education and Training (VET) and Adult Learning team within the OECD Centre for Skills, overseeing the final draft. Support throughout the project was received from El Iza Mohamedou as Head of the Centre for Skills, and Mark Pearson, Deputy Director of the Directorate for Employment, Labour and Social Affairs.

The OECD is very grateful for the inputs received from colleagues at Fundação Itaú para Educação e Cultura, and many others who provided insights during our virtual consultations, and for the feedback received from Manuela Fitzpatrick and Caitlyn Guthrie from the OECD Directorate for Education and Skills.

The OECD is also most grateful to the Gatsby Charitable Foundation for permission to make use of material first published in Field (2021), *A World Without Maps? Assessment in Technical Education, A Report to the Gatsby Foundation*, Gatsby Charitable Foundation, in Chapter 5 of this report.

Table of contents

Foreword	3
Executive summary	6
1 Key insights and recommendations	**8**
Economic and labour market context in Brazil	9
Upper secondary VET in Brazil	12
How Brazil's VET system compares to other countries	14
Summary of the main challenges and recommendations	19
References	25
Note	27
2 Effective strategies for expanding vocational education and training in Brazil	**28**
Making VET work for a diverse group of students	29
Finding VET teachers to support VET expansion	35
Supporting schools in offering relevant VET programmes	37
Conclusions	40
References	41
3 Involvement of employers in the provision of training	**44**
Making the most of work-based learning	45
Designing effective work-based learning opportunities	46
Supporting employers to engage in WBL	52
Conclusions	58
References	58
4 Governance and framework for social partners' involvement in vocational education and training	**62**
Co-ordinating VET policies	63
Systematically involving social partners	66
Conclusions	72
References	73
5 Assessment and certification in vocational education and training	**75**
The role of assessment and certification in vocational education and training	76
Building valid and reliable assessments	80
Assessing the right set of skills at the right time	84
Involving all relevant actors in the assessment process	88

| 5

Using assessment data to support VET policy implementation and quality assurance	90
Conclusions	91
References	92
Annex 5.A. Defining occupational competence for a blacksmith in England: Knowledge, skills and behaviours required	96
Annex 5.B. Assessment in detail: Vocational assessment in Germany in apprenticeship - the example of plumber qualifications	99

FIGURES

Figure 1.1. Trends in total employment and employment share by required skills in Brazil	9
Figure 1.2. Educational attainment of 25-34 year-olds, 2019	10
Figure 1.3. Out of school rate by level of education, 2018	11
Figure 1.4. Enrolment of upper secondary students in VET, 2018	14
Figure 1.5. Distribution of upper secondary vocational students by type of vocational programme (2018)	16
Figure 1.6. Employment rates of 25-34 year-olds, by educational attainment and programme orientation (2019)	17

TABLES

Table 3.1. Comparison of WBL in apprenticeship and school-based programmes	47
Table 4.1. The levels at which there exists an institutional framework for social partner engagement (2007 data)	67
Table 5.1. The relative advantages of standardised and work-embedded tasks in assessment in vocational education and training	83
Table 5.2. The relative advantages of atomistic and holistic approaches to assessment in vocational programmes	85

Follow OECD Publications on:

 http://twitter.com/OECD_Pubs

 http://www.facebook.com/OECDPublications

 http://www.linkedin.com/groups/OECD-Publications-4645871

 http://www.youtube.com/oecdilibrary

OECD Alerts *http://www.oecd.org/oecddirect/*

Executive summary

Brazil launched a major reform of its upper secondary education in 2017. The reform, which is now being implemented, aims to considerably expand provision of initial vocational education and training (VET). The goal is to triple enrolment between 2014-2024. As high-quality VET leads to positive outcomes, the reform of VET in Brazil is a welcome initiative, provided that the expansion of VET is coupled with investments in its quality.

There are three main challenges related to the expansion of VET. First, the reform aims to provide state schools with greater responsibility for the mix of programmes on offer and their content. But the mismatch between VET provision and labour market demand for skills might be a challenge in Brazil as the choice of VET courses is made by VET institutions themselves, with little consideration for the labour market demand needs. Brazil needs to consider how to support schools in their expansion of VET delivery and coordinate provision of different VET programmes locally. Second, the reform expanding VET in schools in Brazil will certainly increase the demand for teachers of VET subjects. To avoid teacher shortages and ensure that VET teachers have relevant and up-to-date skills, many countries have introduced flexible arrangements for qualified employees so that they can teach in their area of expertise without too many entry barriers. In some countries it is also possible to combine a job in industry with some teaching responsibilities. Third, in its expansion plans, Brazil should give careful consideration to the roles that VET can play. VET programmes may be designed to cater to different populations, including those who wish to continue in education and those who are at risk of dropping out. In Brazil, vocational qualifications are awarded to students who complete their academic upper secondary studies. This arrangement may leave less academically oriented students with no qualification if they do not successfully complete their upper secondary education.

The reform of VET in Brazil should be accompanied by an effort of making work-based learning (WBL) a systematic part of VET programmes given the benefits associated with WBL. Provision of training in companies is more cost-effective and can contribute to making the VET offer more relevant to labour market needs. To ensure all VET students can benefit from WBL, including in programmes provided mainly in schools, some countries make WBL mandatory. The benefits from WBL depend on the quality of work placements. Some employers may not feel able to train students, and some are better than others at conducting training. Governments can enhance the training capacity of firms through a wide range of tools, such as promoting training of trainers in companies and facilitating collaboration across companies in the provision of training. Small companies may particularly benefit from measures designed to help with training. Schools can also play an important role in reaching out to employers. Partnerships between schools and local companies facilitate the initial offer of work placements, and the subsequent exchanges between schools and training employers sustain the work placements and ensure that the placements fit effectively into the vocational programmes. But building partnerships between schools and employers is hugely challenging, especially in countries where collaboration between the public and private sector is scarce. To develop WBL in initial VET, Brazil may draw on the experience of employers who already provide work placements to adult learners.

The governance of VET is often complex. Responsibility for VET can be spread across different bodies and levels of governance. Some countries attempt to reduce fragmentation and foster coordination in VET policy by vesting one institution with overarching responsibility over VET and sometimes by creating an independent body whose role is to mediate and represent interests of various stakeholders. The issue of coordination between various decision-makers may also potentially represent a challenge in Brazil. The objective should be to ensure coordination of various provisions, typically organised at the national or regional level, while allowing innovation and flexibility at the local level. A strong VET system involves social partners, typically including employers and trade unions, at all levels where decisions about VET are taken. In some countries, the involvement of social partners is guaranteed by law. Social partners' engagement would typically be strong in apprenticeship systems, whereas in school-based VET it would be less prominent. In Brazil, some VET programmes are already successfully run by employers as part of the Sistema S system. Involvement of Sistema S in the discussion on the what the VET system should look like could help in ensuring the quality of VET.

Reliable assessment and certification mechanisms are crucial in high-quality VET systems to assure that graduates have the required competences. Assessments in the Brazilian VET system should balance different assessment methods. To support reliability, assessments should include some standardised elements, such as written or practical assessment tasks which are the same or very similar for all candidates. However, there is also a need to assess the performance of candidates undertaking realistic work tasks, or pursuing practical projects in the workplace. Full involvement of employers and trade unions enhances the quality of assessment and certification, and improves the credibility of certification. Social partners should be involved fully both in the establishment of new curricula in the expanded VET system in Brazil and in updating existing curricula, as well as in the planning of assessment systems, as employers have the most direct and up to date understanding of required competences. The productive sector might also be usefully involved in undertaking assessments of individual students, as this will add credibility to the consequent certification of occupational competence. While those most closely involved in a training programme, including vocational teachers and employers offering work placements, have direct knowledge of students and their capacities and have a useful input into assessment, involvement of independent actors in assessment would also be helpful. The latter may be less likely to have biases because of any direct interest in the outcome, and are in a stronger position to ensure consistent standards.

1 Key insights and recommendations

This chapter provides an overview of the education system in Brazil and describes main characteristics of its vocational education and training (VET). It discusses a reform of VET that is currently rolled out and that intends to considerably expand provision of VET in Brazil. The chapter points to challenges Brazil may face during the reform process and summarises suggestions for policy advanced in later chapters of the report. Subsequent chapters examine different issues by presenting the topic, describing other countries' approaches, and briefly discussing implications for Brazil.

Economic and labour market context in Brazil

Brazil was only slowly recovering from the previous economic downturn when the pandemic hit in 2020. During a recession young people with limited work experience and vulnerable populations are at a higher risk of being unemployed or excluded from the labour market. Income inequalities have been high in Brazil and the current economic slowdown has exacerbated them further. Education promotes social mobility and boosts economic activities by equipping individuals with knowledge and skills necessary to thrive in the labour market and in other domains of social life. Increasing access to and improving outcomes from education is thus a priority. This report focuses on a specific type of education, mainly vocational education training (VET) in initial schooling, and more precisely how Brazil can expand it and make it more relevant to the labour market.

The structural changes Brazil is facing makes educational reform, including its VET component, even more urgent. In the past, high commodity prices and a favourable demographic situation with a rising working age population boosted economic growth. However, in 2019 the trend was reversed and the share of 15-64 year olds in the total population started to fall. It is expected that the Brazilian population will age faster than the majority of OECD countries and partner economies, and the economic growth generated by the favourable demography will be reversed in the next 25 years (OECD, 2020[1]). Over time, the structure of employment has dramatically changed, with rising demand for higher-level skills. Jobs relying on low skills rapidly declined whereas the share of jobs with high and medium level skills increased (see Figure 1.1) investment in the skills of young people and the current labour force is thus necessary to help the country recover from the recession and boost economic activity.

Figure 1.1. Trends in total employment and employment share by required skills in Brazil

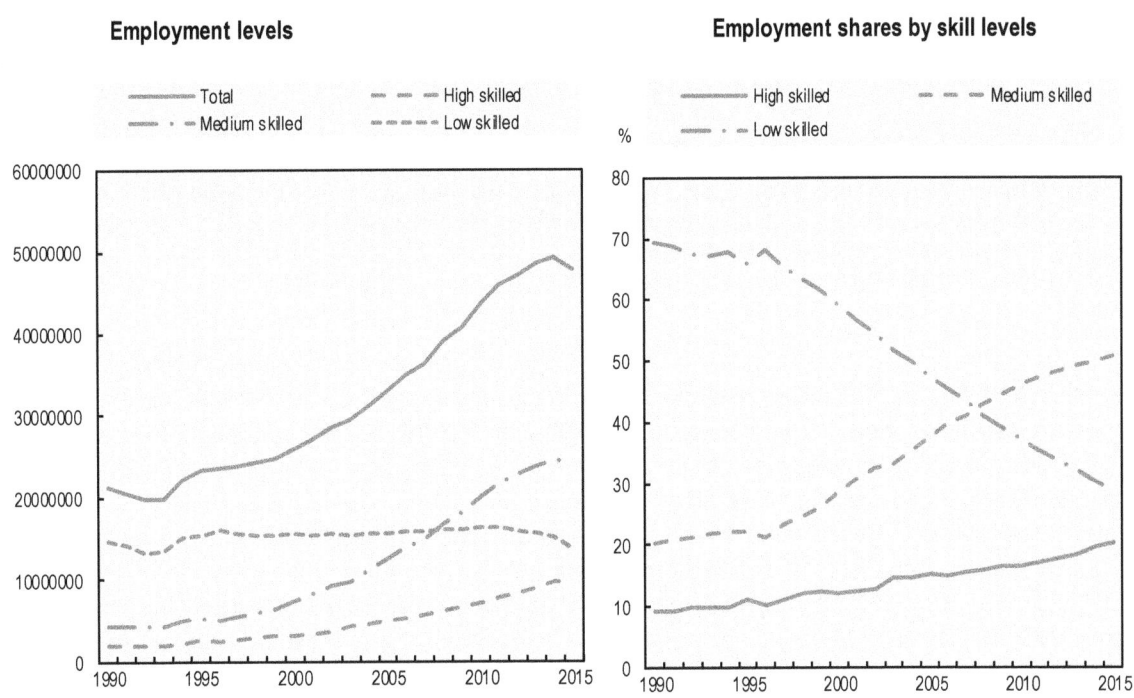

Note: Skill level is defined according to educational attainment of workers: upper secondary not completed (low skilled), secondary completed and tertiary non-completed (medium skilled) and tertiary completed (high skilled).
Source: OECD (2020[1]), *OECD Economic Surveys: Brazil 2020*, https://dx.doi.org/10.1787/250240ad-en.

Brazil managed to increase access to education in recent years but challenges remain. More than 30% of young adults (25-34) lack upper secondary education (OECD, 2020[2]) (Figure 1.2). This is substantially higher than on average across OECD countries (15%). Moreover, a relatively small share of young adults have a tertiary education degree: only 21% of adults aged 25-34 have a tertiary education qualification, compared to 45% across OECD countries on average. The out of school rates (Figure 1.3) remain high with 15% of youth in the official age range staying outside upper secondary education (OECD, 2020[2]).

Figure 1.2. Educational attainment of 25-34 year-olds, 2019

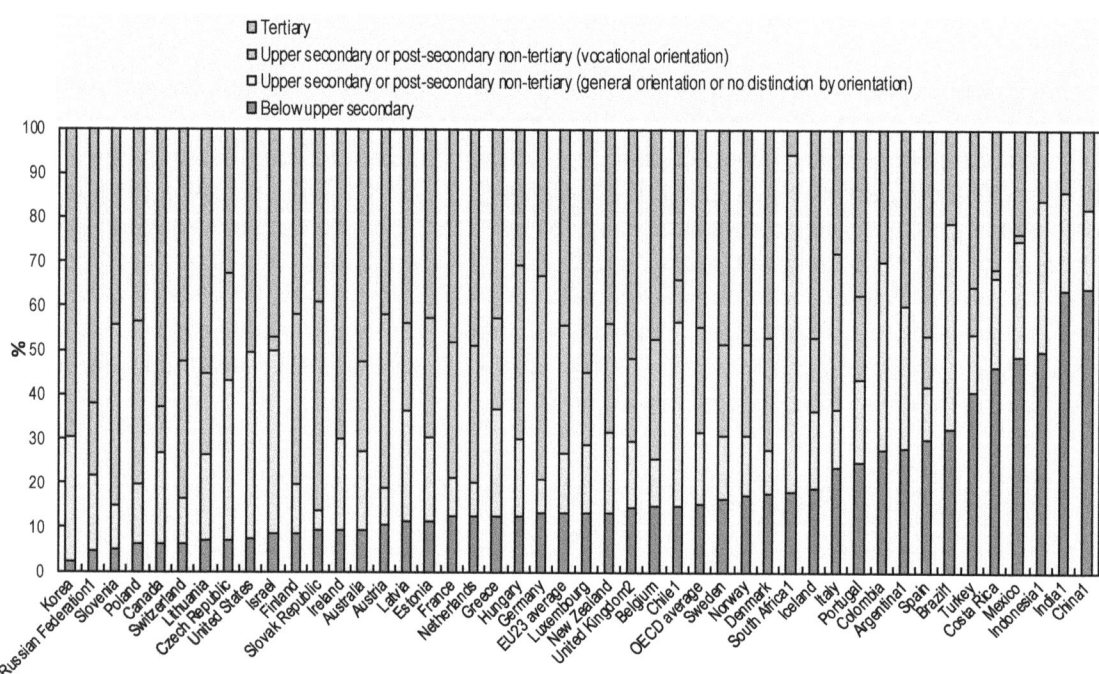

Note: 1 Year of reference differs from 2019. 2. Data for upper secondary attainment include completion of a sufficient volume and standard of programmes that would be classified individually as completion of intermediate upper secondary programmes (12% of adults aged 25-64 are in this group). Countries are ranked in ascending order of the share of 25-34 year-olds who attained below upper secondary education.
Source: OECD (2020[2]), *Education at a Glance 2020: OECD Indicators*, https://doi.org/10.1787/69096873-en.

Young people with low levels of education are at a higher risk of being neither in education nor in employment (NEET). OECD (2020[2]) estimates that young adults (aged 25-29) without upper secondary education are four times more likely to become NEET than those with tertiary education. In Brazil 30% of 20-24 year olds are neither in education nor in employment, which is above the OECD average and higher than in other Latin American countries such as Mexico, Argentina, Costa Rica, Chile and Colombia. Worryingly, over the last 10 years the share of young adults outside education and the labour market increased by 7 percentage points. This may be related to the economic recession that started in the mid-2010s and the sluggish recovery that followed. With the new economic downturn triggered by the pandemic, NEET rates have been increasing (da Silva and Vaz, 2020[3]). Measures promoting economic recovery and reducing social inequalities may include improving access and completion of upper secondary education, facilitating the transition of young people from school to work, and increasing the skills of the existing workforce. Vocational education and training (VET), currently underdeveloped in Brazil, can be used to this end. (See Box 1.1 for the definition of vocational education and training.)

Box 1.1. How vocational education and training is defined

Vocational education is designed for learners to acquire the knowledge, skills and competencies specific to a particular occupation, trade, or class of occupations or trades. Vocational education may have work-based components. Successful completion of such programmes leads to labour market-relevant vocational qualifications acknowledged as occupationally oriented by the relevant national authorities and/or the labour market.

By contrast, general education programmes are designed to develop learners' general knowledge, skills and competencies, as well as literacy and numeracy skills, often to prepare participants for more advanced education programmes at the same or a higher ISCED level and to lay the foundation for lifelong learning. Such programmes are typically school- or college-based. General education includes education programmes that are designed to prepare participants for entry into vocational education but do not prepare for employment in a particular occupation, trade or class of occupations or trades, nor lead directly to a labour-market relevant qualification

Source: Kis, V. (2020[4]), "Improving evidence on VET: Comparative data and indicators", *OECD Social, Employment and Migration Working Papers*, No. 250, , https://dx.doi.org/10.1787/d43dbf09-en; OECD (2017[5]), *OECD Handbook for Internationally Comparative Education Statistics: Concepts, Standards, Definitions and Classifications*, https://dx.doi.org/10.1787/9789264279889-en.

Figure 1.3. Out of school rate by level of education, 2018

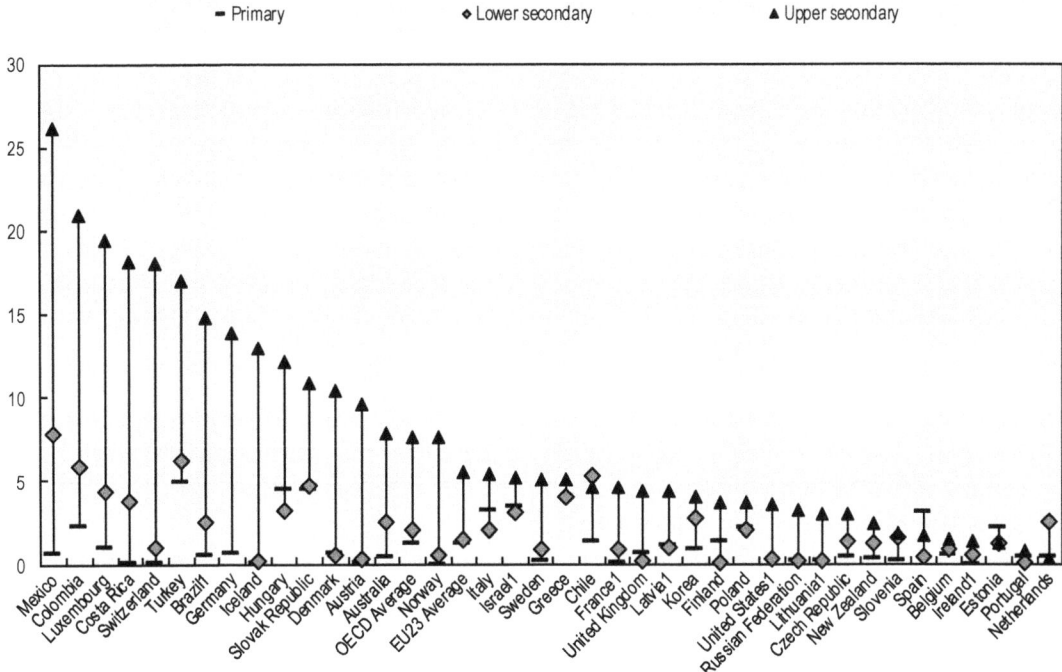

Note: The source for population data is the UOE data collection for demographic data (Eurostat/DEM) instead of the United Nations Population Division (UNPD). Out of school rate (one year before primary, lower secondary and upper secondary education) refers to a proportion of children and young people in the official age range for the given level of education who are not enrolled in primary, lower secondary and upper secondary education (UNESCO, 2021[6]).
Source: OECD (2020[2]), *Education at a Glance 2020: OECD Indicators*, https://dx.doi.org/10.1787/69096873-en.

Upper secondary VET in Brazil

Brazil's education system in a nutshell

Brazil divides its education system into basic and higher education levels. The basic level includes: early childhood education (ECEC); primary and lower secondary education (*ensino fundamental*); and upper secondary education (*ensino médio*). Education is compulsory from the age of four until the end of upper secondary education. Enrolment in primary education is near universal, but lower secondary enrolment rates are still low by international standards. Access to public education is free at all levels, including tertiary education provided by publicly funded universities. However, in Brazil many students are enrolled in private higher education institutions typically charging tuition fees, with over three-quarters of bachelor's students enrolled in private institutions (OECD, 2019[7]).

Brazil is a highly decentralised country. It has a three-level federal system of government, including the federal government and federative entities (26 states, the Federal District and 5 569 municipalities). States and municipalities have direct responsibility for ECEC and primary education, states are the main providers of lower and upper secondary education, and the federal government is mainly responsible for higher education (OECD, 2021[8]). VET schools can be run by the federal government, states, municipalities and private entities. The make-up of different providers depends on the type of VET provision (see below for an overview of the different types of provision). For example, 62% of students completing integrated initial VET programmes were educated in institutions run by the federal government and only 3% attended privately run institutions. In initial concomitant VET more than 60% of students attended private institutions (including Sistema S) and only 26% received education in federal schools (Brasil Ministério da Educação/Conselho Nacional de Educação, 2021[9]).

The federal government sets national standards and overall objectives for the country; it directly manages some institutions including the federal universities and vocational federal schools; co-ordinates education policies across the different levels of government; and provides technical and financial assistance to states and municipalities. The Ministry of Education (*Ministério da Educação*, MEC) evaluates the education system through i) the National Institute of Educational Studies and Research Anísio Teixeira (*Instituto Nacional de Estudos e Pesquisas Educacionais Anísio Teixeira*, INEP), whose focus is primarily on pre-tertiary education; and ii) the Foundation for the Co-ordination of Improvement of Higher Education Personnel (*Coordenação de Aperfeiçoamento de Pessoal de Nível Superior*, CAPES), which focuses on higher education. In collaboration with state and municipal governments, the Ministry of Education determines curricular guidelines to be taught at schools. The responsibility for upper secondary VET in Brazil is divided between the Federal Government and the state governments. (OECD, 2021[8]).

In addition, there are several associated bodies with diverse responsibilities in the education system:

- The National Council of Education (*Conselho Nacional de Educação*, CNE) is a collegiate body to the Ministry of Education that is responsible for advising and monitoring the design and implementation of national education policy. It ensures the participation of the Brazilian society in education policy development and improvement.
- The National Education Development Fund (*Fundo Nacional de Desenvolvimento da Educação*, FNDE) is a semi-autonomous body responsible for resource allocation and providing technical support to states and municipalities.

At upper secondary level there are three main VET pathways in Brazil

Upper secondary VET programmes in Brazil are attended by young people (typical age of completion of lower-secondary education is 15) who continue from lower to upper secondary education. These initial upper secondary VET programmes give access to tertiary education. Initial VET in Brazil can be provided in two ways (Brasil Ministério da Educação/Conselho Nacional de Educação, 2021[9]):

- *Integrated.* Students can follow the so-called 'integrated programmes' where vocational and academic content is part of one curriculum, and all the courses are delivered by the same institution. Students pass one final exam at the end of their upper secondary education.
- *Concomitant.* Vocational curriculum is separated from the academic content, with students registering separately for academic and vocational programmes. Students can receive all their classes in one institution, or they may need to attend a different institution to follow VET courses and sit two different final exams (Kauer, 2015[10]).

Upper secondary VET is also available after the completion of upper secondary education (obtaining of an upper secondary diploma). It is called consecutive VET.

- In *consecutive* VET, students embark on upper secondary VET programmes ending with a technician certificate after obtaining an upper secondary diploma. Participants in these VET programmes are typically older than those in initial upper-secondary VET, and many have already acquired some work experience (Kauer, 2015[10]).

In 2020, among all the VET upper secondary students: 50% were in *consecutive* VET provision, 37% in initial *integrated* VTE, and 13% in *concomitant* VET (INEP, 2021[11]). Upper secondary VET leads to the qualification of *Técnico Nível Médio*. The most popular VET programmes are in health, industry and management (OECD, 2014[12]). VET programmes are provided by public institutions (such as federal, state and municipal schools) and private providers, with private institutions enrolling more than half of all upper secondary VET students. Private providers include private vocational schools and institutions of the Sistema S. The Brazilian Sistema S is a group of 10 non-profit private institutions specific to an economical sector and carrying out private activities of public interest. Among others, they provide professional and technical education, to meet the demand for qualified workers (Souza et al., 2015[13]). Two of the Sistema S institutions: SENAI (National Service of Industrial Education) and SENAC (National Commercial Training Service) cater to 38% of the VET students enrolled in private institutions. They provide mainly consecutive VET programmes and some vocational courses in initial concomitant VET. Sistema S institutions may charge fees for some of their services and activities. However, a significant share of their revenue comes from collection of mandatory taxes over payrolls from firms in the sectors they are relative to (Souza et al., 2015[13]). According to the agreement with the federal government, SENAI and SENAC must allocate two-thirds of their revenues from compulsory taxation to the provision of free professional and technical education programs (Souza et al., 2015[13]).

Some initial upper-secondary VET programmes are highly selective and serve mostly as an entry pathway into tertiary education. For example, 38 of the 50 public schools with the highest results on upper secondary tests (ENEM – *Exame National do Ensino Médio*) in Brazil in 2008 were vocational schools. Students may therefore opt for VET not because they want to prepare for a specific profession but because they strive for a good quality education that increase their chances of getting a place at university. According to Kauer (2015[10]), it is mainly the fully integrated initial VET that attracts students from more affluent families. This is less the case in concomitant initial and consecutive VET, which are more likely to attract students from more modest backgrounds seeking labour market relevant qualifications that should help them obtain quality jobs.

Involvement of social partners in initial VET is weak, aside from various consecutive VET programmes run by employers' organisations. Students in initial VET receive their vocational training in school workshops and the majority of the VET schools do not collaborate with employers. One of the reasons for this separation between schools and the world of work is that there are legal obstacles preventing schools from forging stronger partnerships with employers. For example, public schools are not allowed to offer apprenticeships. Given very limited input from social partners in initial VET, employers often perceive it as irrelevant (Itaú Educação e Trabalho, 2021[14]). In comparison to some other countries with strong initial VET systems and to some consecutive VET programmes in Brazil, there is lack of a structure promoting collaboration between education providers and companies.

Post-secondary VET opportunities are limited in Brazil. Examples from other countries, such as Switzerland and Sweden, show that postsecondary VET pathways often allow upper secondary VET graduates to continue in education. Lack of postsecondary options may decrease the attractiveness of VET to students.

How Brazil's VET system compares to other countries

Enrolment in VET

In comparison to other OECD countries and partner economies, young people in Brazil who are in upper secondary education follow mainly academic paths. In 2018, only 10% of upper secondary students pursued VET paths, which was a smaller share than in most OECD countries (see Figure 1.4). On average across OECD countries, 37% of upper secondary students were in VET programmes. In Brazil, VET is more common among adult learners. In 2018, one in five students aged 25 and above were enrolled in upper secondary VET programmes (OECD, 2020[2]).

Figure 1.4. Enrolment of upper secondary students in VET, 2018

Full- and part-time students enrolled in public and private institutions, age 15-19

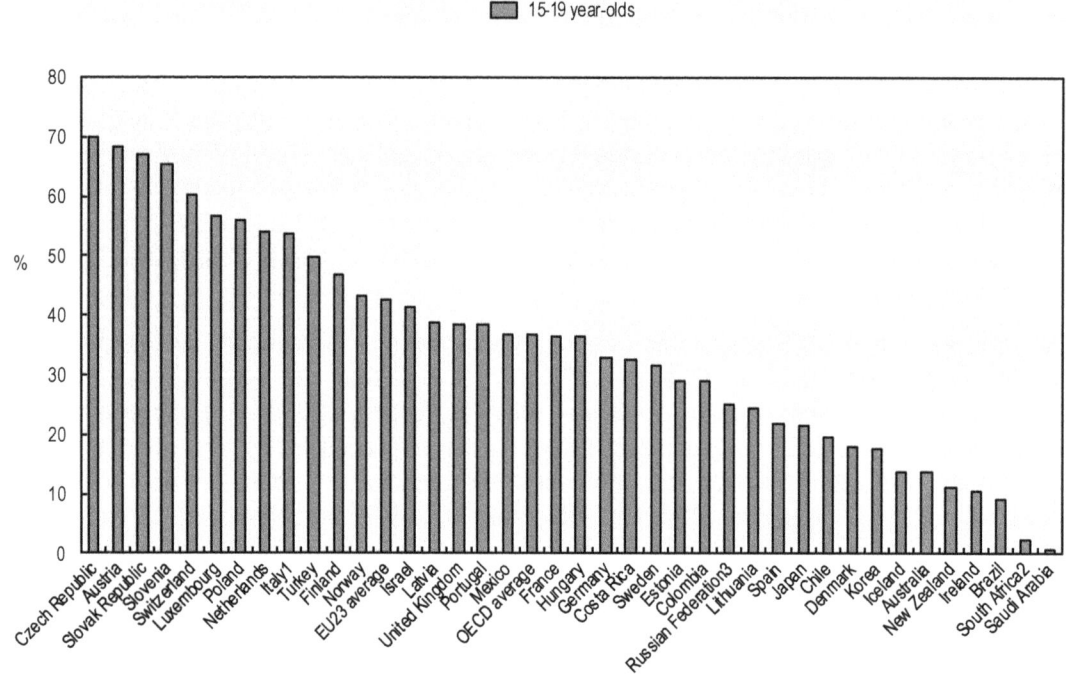

Note: 1. Includes post-secondary non-tertiary programmes. 2. Year of reference 2017. 3. Excludes part of upper secondary vocational programmes. Countries and economies are ranked in descending order of the highest share of upper secondary enrolment in vocational education and training programmes.
Source: OECD (2020[2]), *Education at a Glance 2020: OECD Indicators*, https://dx.doi.org/10.1787/69096873-en.

In a high-quality VET system, students share their time between school where they receive general education (history, mathematics, literature), and workplaces where they can acquire and apply their knowledge and skills in real work situations. Hence, vocational programmes typically lead to a recognised qualification, and involve a structured mix of:

- Work based learning (WBL): work placements with an employer that leads to the development of new skills (through participation in, and/or observation of work, under the supervision of an employer). In programmes with longer periods of WBL students typically contribute with some productive work.
- Off-the-job education and training at school, college or other educational and training provider involving no or limited productive work.

The distinction between academic and vocational learning can sometimes be challenging as the two can be provided at the same time. For example, students in electricity programmes may learn about laws of physics in an applied way while building electrical system in workshops; and students in construction need to know geometry to build a house that is not going to collapse.

In Brazil, work based learning is not part of initial upper secondary VET (see Figure 1.5). On average across OECD countries, one in three upper secondary VET students are in programmes with a substantial WBL component, and in a number of OECD countries all VET students have access to WBL. In Brazil restrictive health and safety regulations prevent companies from providing training to minors on company sites (OECD, 2020[1]). For example, legal restrictions contributed to a closedown of an upper secondary vocational programme with training provided in training centres of a car manufacturing company (OECD, 2020[1]). While regulations are important to protect the safety of minors, any reform of upper secondary VET should ensure that WBL can be part of the programme.

Brazil is not unique in having limited VET provision in initial upper secondary education and a parallel training system run by employers. In Peru, for example, industry sectors run their own schools providing technical skills in the relevant area. Most of the time they are independent of the Ministry of Education and are operated by the corresponding ministry. For example, schools of the *Servicio Nacional de Capacitación para la Industria de la Construcción* (SENCICO) are operated by the Ministry of Housing. They are funded with tuition fees and sometimes employer levies (McCarthy and Musset, 2016[15]).

Figure 1.5. Distribution of upper secondary vocational students by type of vocational programme (2018)

Full- and part-time students enrolled in public and private institutions

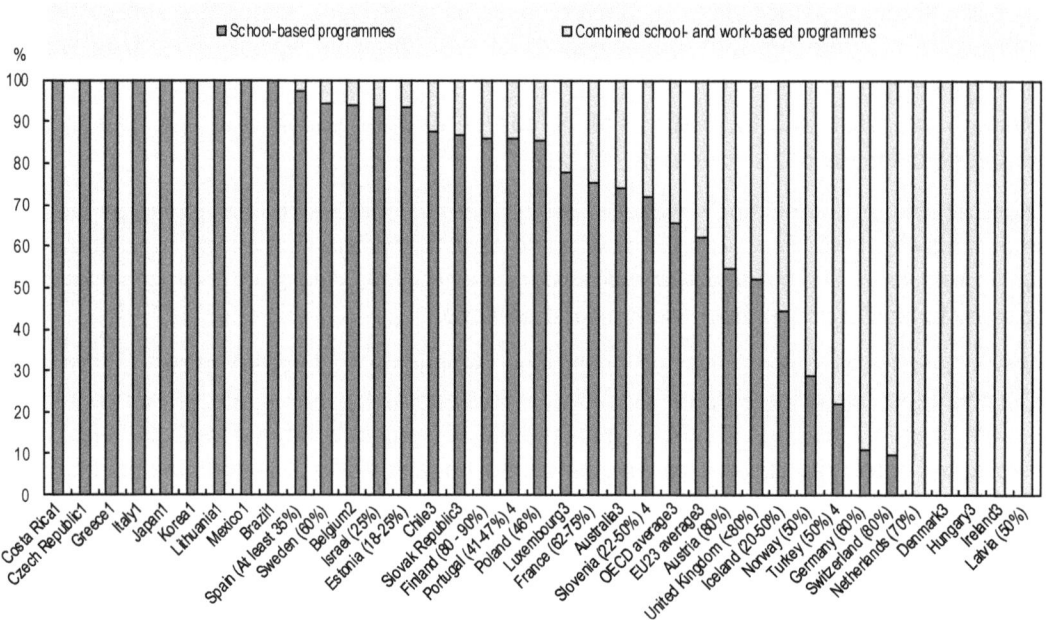

Note: Figures in parentheses refer to the most typical duration of the work-based component as a percentage of the total programme duration for combined school- and work-based programmes. For example, in Germany, more than 98% of students in combined school- and work-based programmes are enrolled in a programme where the duration of the work component accounts for about 60% of the total programme duration.
1. Data on typical duration of the work-based component are not applicable because the category does not apply; 2.The most typical duration of the work-based component is at least 46% for the Flemish Community of Belgium and 60% for the French Community of Belgium; 3. Data on the most typical duration of the work-based component are missing; 4. The share of students enrolled in combined school- and work-based programmes as a percentage of all student enrolled in upper secondary vocational education is estimated based on the results of the INES ad-hoc survey on VET.
Source: OECD (2020[2]), *Education at a Glance 2020: OECD Indicators*, https://dx.doi.org/10.1787/b35a14e5-en.

Labour market outcomes of VET students

In countries with high-quality VET systems, upper secondary VET programmes provide good employment prospects for their graduates. International evidence demonstrates that young people who completed upper secondary VET have better labour market opportunities upon completion than their counterparts from academic programmes who do not continue to tertiary education (see Figure 1.6). On average across OECD countries, 83% of 25-34 year-olds with an upper secondary VET qualification (as the highest qualifications) are in employment compared to 73% of those with general upper secondary education[1] (OECD, 2020[2]).

As discussed above, in Brazil 90% of upper secondary students are in general programmes, but only a minority of them progress to higher education. Only around one in five of upper secondary completers pursue education at a higher level, with the other 80% or 15 million of young adults entering the labour market with some general upper secondary education but without specific occupational training. In OECD countries on average, 30% of 20-24 year-olds are enrolled in tertiary education (bachelor's degree and above) as compared to 21% in Brazil (OECD, 2020[2]). Over the last thirty years the share of low-skill jobs decreased drastically in Brazil, whereas middle skilled and to some extent high skilled employment expanded (see Figure 1.1). Currently, half of all jobs require middle level skills, suggesting that the demand for upper secondary graduates (which are associated with middle skilled employment), is high. However, a survey carried out among Brazilian employers revealed that in 2018 more than half of them complained about applicants lacking required skills or experience. A further 20% pointed to weak soft skills among candidates (OECD, 2020[1]). Expanded and strengthened VET system can help ensure that upper secondary students develop the right skills for these middle-skill jobs.

Figure 1.6. Employment rates of 25-34 year-olds, by educational attainment and programme orientation (2019)

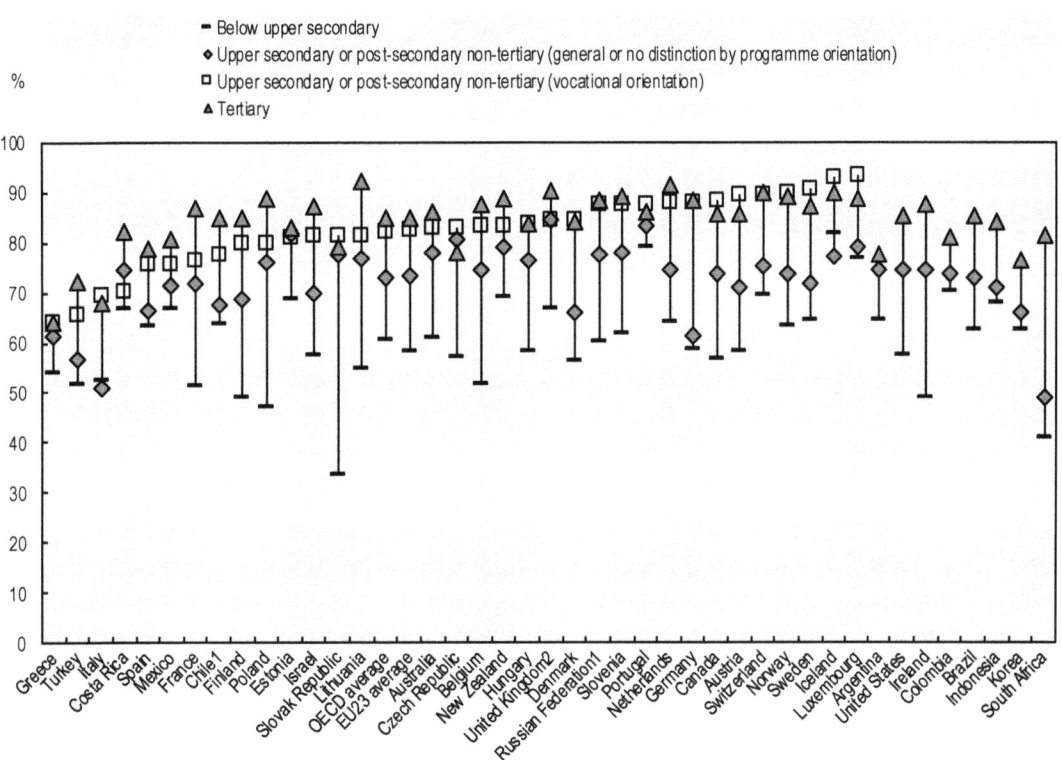

Note: 1. Year of reference differs from 2019. 2. Data for upper secondary attainment include completion of a sufficient volume and standard of programmes that would be classified individually as completion of intermediate upper secondary programmes (12% of adults aged 25-64 are in this group).
Source: OECD (2020[2]), *Education at a Glance 2020: OECD Indicators*, https://dx.doi.org/10.1787/b35a14e5-en.

Reforming the Brazilian VET system

To address the challenges described above, Brazil adopted in 2017 a reform of its upper secondary education. The reform is now being implemented. However, the speed and breadth of the implementation varies across national sub-units (Salas, 2021[16]). Box 1.2 summarise main elements of the reform.

> **Box 1.2. 2017 reform of upper-secondary education in Brazil**
>
> The reform of upper secondary education aims to improve quality, offer more choice to students and make upper secondary education more attractive and engaging. The reform reduces the number of mandatory subjects to be taught and increases class time. In the reformed system, student will follow a common core programme (including mandatory Portuguese and mathematics in all years) and chose one or more options in the following areas: languages; mathematics; natural sciences; human and social sciences; technical and professional training. Education networks, together with schools, have more flexibility over curricula and programme offer (OECD, 2021[8]).
>
> In the area of VET, the reform aims to considerably expand provision of initial VET. The objective is to triple the enrolment between 2014-2024. Vocational education is no longer a separate track, but has instead become an optional component of students' upper secondary studies. It also intends to provide more flexibility to students by diversifying the options students can choose from, and providing schools with more opportunities to adjust their programmes and curricula to local needs. The reform facilitates recruitment of vocational teachers by allowing schools to hire professionals with relevant work experience but without teacher training (OECD, 2021[8]).
>
> Source: OECD (2021[8]), *Education in Brazil. An International Perspective*, https://doi.org/10.1787/60a667f7-en.

As high-quality VET leads to positive outcomes, the planned expansion of VET in Brazil is a welcome reform, provided that this expansion is coupled with investments in quality. There is no system that fits all. The design of VET programmes differs depending on their objectives and the population they serve. However, regardless of the exact structure of VET some characteristics define a good quality VET system. One key characteristic of good quality VET is that it is recognised and supported by employers.

The remainder of this report describes building blocks of good quality VET systems drawing on country examples. This report focuses on initial VET, which in Brazil refers to initial integrated and concomitant pathways. Consecutive VET is not one of the choices available to students on entry to the upper secondary phase of education, so it plays a very different role in the education and skills system. While this report does not concern itself with consecutive VET, providing a full picture of VET provision in Brazil is important as the coexistence of different provisions may lead to co-ordination and collaboration challenges. In addition, good practices found in consecutive VET, such as the involvement of social partners (Sistema S), could potentially be emulated in initial VET.

The remainder of this chapter summarises the key findings from the report. Chapter 2 discusses how academic and vocational content can be combined in VET programmes to serve diverse population, how Brazil could handle recruitment of VET teachers, and finally how schools can be supported to provide good quality VET given the planned expansion of school-based VET. Involvement of employers in provision of work-based learning is a topic of Chapter 3. Chapter 4 addresses different governance arrangements for VET and social partner's involvement in the governance of the VET system. Finally, Chapter 5 describes assessment and certification in VET, with a particular focus on employer engagement in these processes.

Summary of the main challenges and recommendations

What are the avenues for expansion of VET system in Brazil?

Key issues and challenges

VET can serve different populations. VET programmes may be designed to prepare students for entry into the labour market and/or to continue in education. There are also programmes that target those who dropped out from school or are at risk of dropping out (Kis, 2020[4]). Designing a system that meets these different purposes can be challenging. Schools may not always have the right incentives to offer relevant programmes. Provision of VET may pose many challenges to schools in Brazil, as few have experience with VET provision. VET programmes are more expensive than academic ones, as workshop equipment can be costly. Unless schools are supported, there is a risk they would provide programmes in areas that are less expensive to provide but not necessarily in occupations in which labour market demand is high.

The attractiveness and quality of VET depends on its teachers. OECD (2021[17]) shows that many countries face acute VET teacher shortages. Aging of the teacher population and the low attractiveness of the profession are some of the factors to blame.

Solutions and strategies to address the issues

Balancing academic and vocational content

VET programmes prepare young people for jobs but also for continuing in education. To this end, they combine vocational and academic content. Academic content (such as mathematics, language) that is required to continue at higher-level programmes can either be integrated into the VET programmes or be an optional add-on. Within VET provision, some programmes may be academically more demanding than others.

- *Integrated VET and academic content*: Completion of both vocational and academic qualifications may require extra effort and time from students, as in fact students work towards a double qualification.
- *Add-on programmes*: Alternatively, VET programmes may not automatically offer eligibility for higher education but VET students or graduates who would like to continue into higher-level programmes have the option of taking additional academic courses on top of a vocational qualification.
- *Diversified VET programmes with different academic requirements*: Differences in the target population can be reflected in the content and objectives of different programmes. To diversify provision, some VET programmes can be more academically demanding than others can.

Providing special forms of VET targeted at youth at risk

VET can be an attractive option for less academically oriented students. Some countries offer VET programmes (typically apprenticeship) of shorter duration to students at risk of dropping out. In strong school systems, those facing the greatest challenges receive extra coaching to help them succeed. So as these programmes are not seen as a low status option, they should seamlessly articulate with higher levels of education. In Austria, for example, integrative VET programmes (Integrative Berufsausbildung, IBA) target young people with special needs (two-thirds of participants), disabled youth and those without a school-leaving certificate.

Finding VET teachers to support expansion

Recruitment of VET teachers can be difficult as VET teachers have to be acquainted with the area of specialisation (e.g. construction, electronics, and hairdressing) and at the same time be able to effectively transfer their knowledge and skills to young people. Many countries, including Brazil, have introduced flexible arrangements for qualified employees so that they can teach in their area of expertise without too many entry barriers. These measures help address teacher shortages and ensure that those teaching VET subjects are abreast of the recent development in the relevant industry. To facilitate entry to the professions, many countries allow newcomers with industry background to complete a teaching qualification while on the job or to shorten the training programme. In some countries, it is also possible to combine a job in industry with some teaching responsibilities.

Supporting schools in offering relevant VET programmes

The organisation of the school network and the programmes provided by schools ideally take into account the cost of provision, students' preferences and labour market needs. Countries take various approaches to ensuring that the offer and organisation of VET satisfies the different needs in a cost-effective way:

- *Concentration of provision*: By concentrating provision and merging schools, the cost of providing VET programmes could be lowered and/or quality improved, as the fixed cost associated with running a VET programme, is, within reason, independent of the number of students. For example, if there are three schools in the area offering a similar VET programme, all three schools have to equip workshops and hire VET teachers to run the programme.
- *Sharing facilities*: Training centres or workshops can serve students from different schools in one local area.
- *Schools specialisation*: Specialisation of schools, focusing provision on just one field, such as health care, has many advantages, including that it can lower the cost of provision and facilitate participation of students in work placements with employers. One option is for students to start their upper secondary VET programme in their local school, with an emphasis on more general education and training, and then attend for a couple of weeks a more specialised VET school in their second or third year. This would reduce the potential problems associated with younger students moving far from home and spending long hours on commuting, or having to live away from home.

The implications for Brazil

The Brazilian reform aims to expand provision of school-based VET and provide public schools with larger responsibility over the mix of programmes on offer and their content. But the mismatch between VET provision and labour market demand for skills is a challenge in Brazil as the choice of VET courses is decided mainly by VET institutions with little consideration for the labour market side (Souza et al., 2015[13]). Brazil needs to consider how to support schools and coordinate provision of different VET programmes locally. Moreover, the reform expanding VET in schools will certainly increase the demand for teachers of VET subjects. Flexible recruitment of skilled employees is one of the solutions to avoid VET teacher shortages and ensure that teachers have up to date industry-relevant skills. This option has already been introduced in Brazil, and should be further encouraged and supported. Many countries allow entry of skilled employees into VET profession. However, VET teachers without pedagogical training need to be strongly encouraged to complete teacher training while on the job.

Brazil may encourage providing various VET programmes or tracks that cater to the needs of different target populations. In Brazil, upper secondary vocational qualifications are awarded to those who complete their academic upper secondary studies. This arrangement may leave less academically oriented students with no qualification if they do not successfully complete their upper secondary education. Inclusion of demanding academic content in all VET programmes can be detrimental to less academically oriented students and may contribute to higher dropout rates. States that have already introduced such programmes should evaluate their outcomes, with good practices scaled up across the country.

How to promote provision of work place training to students by employers?

Key issues and challenges

Training with employers or work based learning (WBL) is a key element of vocational education and training. It yields benefits to students and employers. It is also less costly than provision of training in school workshops. However, many countries struggle with securing enough training places with employers. Schools can play an important role in reaching out to employers. Partnerships between schools and local companies facilitate the initial offer of work placements, and the subsequent exchanges between schools and training employers sustain the work placements and ensure that the placements fit effectively into the vocational programme. However, building partnerships between schools and employers is hugely challenging, especially in countries where collaboration between the public and private sector is scarce.

The benefits from WBL depend on the quality of work placements. High quality work placements develop useful skills in student and are run by trainers who know how to work with young people. Employers may be reluctant to introduce some of the measures that aim to strengthening quality as they increase the cost of training provision.

Solutions and strategies to address the issues

Making work-based learning with employers mandatory

To ensure all VET students can benefit from WBL, including in programmes provided mainly in schools, some countries made WBL mandatory. A school can only offer a programme if there are enough training places. For example in Sweden, all students in VET programmes lasting 3 years should spend at least 15 weeks in company training.

Supporting schools in reaching out to employers

Individual schools may need support in developing links with employers and the capacity to foster WBL. Sometimes this support may come from organised bodies. For example, in the Netherlands, all companies offering work placements (both in apprenticeship and school-based programmes) have to be accredited by the Foundation for Cooperation between Vocational Education, Training and the Labour Market (SBB) – a body involving various stakeholders including employers and trade unions (ECBO, 2016[18]).

Helping companies to train

Some employers may not feel able to train students, and some are better than others at conducting training. Training capacity is typically less developed in small companies that do not have dedicated training arrangements. Small companies may therefore particularly benefit from measures designed to help with training. Governments can enhance the training capacity of firms through a wide range of tools.

- Training of trainers: To ensure company employees who are responsible for training of students have the capacity to convey knowledge and develop skills in students, some countries require or encourage trainers to take up an appropriate training. Governments may also facilitate networking among employers to share knowledge and experience on how best to support students and develop their skills. In Norway, the Norwegian Directorate for Education offers free resources for apprentice instructors on their website, including short movies showing how instruction can be carried out in practice (Norwegian Directorate for Education and Training, 2011[19]).

- Companies working together to provide training: To support employers that on their own would not be able to deliver WBL, many countries have arrangements that allow employers to share responsibility for it. In Germany for example, various models exist for employers to share the responsibility for training an apprentice, including small enterprises working together as part of a training consortium.
- Financial incentives: Countries provide subsidies and tax breaks to encourage employers to offer training to students. In some countries the cost of training is shared across employers who contribute to a training levy fund. In countries without a tradition of employers' engagement in VET, schools play a more active role in initiating and organising work placements and sometimes in funding. For example, in Estonia schools can transfer funding to enterprises to cover salary costs of workplace supervisors.

The implications for Brazil?

Expansion of VET in Brazil should be accompanied by an effort of making WBL a systematic part of VET programmes given the benefits associated with WBL. Provision of training in companies is more cost-effective and can contribute to making the VET offer more relevant to labour market needs. To develop WBL in initial VET, Brazil may draw on experience of employers who already provide work placements to adult learners. In Brazil, there are limited WBL opportunities in initial VET, but in programmes for adults, often run by social partners, WBL is more common. Brazil has well established sectoral training levy funds. It can be explored if and how this experience can be used to promote WBL in upper secondary VET.

Helping employers to meet various requirements and to 'teach' them how to train students may be necessary to expand WBL opportunities in Brazil. Supporting training of trainers and encouraging employers to work together are some of the solutions.

Who is responsible for VET and how to involve employers into VET policy?

Key issues and challenges

The governance of VET is often complex. VET caters to different student populations, such as young people in schools and adults returning to education, and spans across a range of sectors. Consequently, responsibility for VET can be spread across different bodies and levels of governance. Co-ordination of VET policies is important, but should not eliminate local and school autonomy in VET. However, decentralisation typically results in a lot of variation if the outcomes are very much dependent on individual institutions. Ideally, national prerogatives are combined with local freedom whereby schools can often adapt the content to the local labour markets. Combining these multiple interests can sometimes be difficult.

Involvement of social partners in VET policy yields many benefits but can be difficult to establish. Strong VET systems, drawing on social partner engagement, yield benefits to employers by increasing the pool of qualified labour, and benefit students by facilitating their transition to skilled employment. Building social partners' involvement is easier in countries where employer organisations (e.g. industry chambers in Germany) exist already. In Brazil, employer associations exist and are in some cases well organised (e.g. Sistema S), which should facilitate building their engagement in VET.

Solutions and strategies to address the issues

Strengthening collaboration

Countries attempt to reduce fragmentation and foster co-ordination in VET policy by:

- Vesting one institution with overarching responsibility over VET. In a federal context, a number of countries balance decentralisation with strong federal institutions in the domain of vocational education and training. For example, in Viet Nam the legislation simplified the previously scattered VET landscape and consolidated most responsibilities for the VET system under the Ministry of Labour, Invalids and Social Affairs.
- Fostering collaboration between different bodies and levels, and sometimes creating an independent body which role is to mediate and represent interests of various stakeholders. In Malaysia, for example, a national TVET Council (MTVET) was set up at the end of 2020 in an effort to bring more co-ordination into the scattered landscape, which has programmes governed by eleven ministries and delivered by private, public and state government VET institutions.

Different measures are not exclusive, i.e. a country may vest one level of governance (e.g. federal authority) with more responsibilities and at the same time create independent bodies facilitating collaboration.

Involving social partners

A strong VET system involves social partners at all levels where decisions about VET are taken. Social partners are often organised by sectors and decide or advise on corresponding VET programmes. For example, social partners representing the construction sector provide input in the design of VET programmes in construction. The influence of social partners can be simply advisory or consultative, or alternatively can involve full decision-making. In some countries, law guarantees the involvement of social partners. Social partners' engagement would typically be strong in apprenticeship systems, whereas in school based VET it would be less prominent.

The implications for Brazil

Some forms of co-ordination between different levels of governance and existing systems can be envisaged. The issue of co-ordination between various decision-makers may potentially represent a challenge in Brazil as VET schools are run by a range of bodies, including the federal government, states, municipalities, private providers from Sistema S and other private providers (Itaú Educação e Trabalho, 2021[14]). Local autonomy is particularly important in large and diverse countries such as Brazil as it is highly unlikely that one set of rules and standards would suit all localities. Ideally, national/regional prerogatives are combined with local freedom whereby schools can often adapt the content to the local labour markets. Therefore, the objective should be to ensure co-ordination of various provisions, typically organised at the national or regional level, while allowing innovation and flexibility at the local level.

Brazil may start with creating a few VET programmes in collaboration with social partners (that can be scaled up if successful). This would involve, for example, setting up collaboration between schools and large companies from a specific sector that would advise on the content of VET subjects and offer work placements to students in relevant programmes. Employers (Sistema S) already run some VET programmes, and many of these programmes are associated with positive labour market outcomes. Involvement of Sistema S in the current reform and in discussions on what the VET system should look like could help in ensuring the quality of VET.

How can assessment and certification contribute to the development of a strong VET system in Brazil?

Key issues and challenges

Effective assessment is a necessary element of a strong VET system. VET programmes aim to provide graduates with the competences necessary to do specific jobs, and with the certification which assures employers that graduates have those competences. Summative assessment ensures that the required competences have been acquired by graduates. The confidence of employers in VET programmes depends, among other factors, on the quality of assessment systems. If the social partners are fully involved in the development of VET programmes and qualifications, and in the assessments, that will enhance the credibility of the associated certifications. For example in apprenticeship in England, employers take the lead in establishing each apprenticeship qualification, through 'Trailblazer' groups led by employers, which identify the competences required for a job. The same groups also establish an 'assessment plan' setting out in some detail how apprentices are to be assessed at the end of each programme.

There are many dilemmas in designing and implementing VET assessments. Should they be standardised, achieving reliability by ensuring that every candidate faces the same assessment tasks? Or should, alternatively, assessment rely on authentic work challenges and projects, which will vary from candidate to candidate? Should assessment list all the required competences and test them one by one, or, instead, should occupational competence be assessed in the round? Can we rely entirely on an assessment at the end of a training programme, or should that be buttressed with periodic partial assessments undertaken throughout the programme? Can local vocational teachers and providers be trusted to undertake assessment, or do we need independent assessors?

Solutions and strategies to address these issues

Balancing consistency and flexibility

There is a need for some balance between a standardised assessment delivering full reliability, and an assessment based on authentic working practice. Consistent standards in assessment are supported by standardised assessments, as in national examinations. But in the productive sector, ability to do the job is assessed most directly by looking at how well candidates perform authentic work tasks. This might mean, for example, not just undertaking a standard task like fixing a leaking pipe in the case of a plumber, but also negotiating with a client, diagnosing the plumbing fault, working and communicating with other artisans, costing and scheduling the repair task, and dealing with unexpected vocational, practical and human challenges in the course of the work. In upper secondary VET programmes in the Netherlands, for example, workplace projects are conducted within a workplace over a period of around six weeks, and school and workplace trainers normally undertake the assessment and grading.

Assessing overall competence

Assessments need to address both individual competences, and overall occupational competence. Occupational competence involves both mastery of a whole set of individual elements of knowledge and skills, and the overarching capacity to make use all of these competences to solve workplace challenges. In Luxembourg, for example, the summative assessment in apprenticeship includes a module-by-module assessment of the programme, as well as an assessment of a project associated with a simulated or real working situation, undertaken over a period of up to 24 hours.

Ensuring a degree of independence in assessment

Independence in assessment is designed to remove bias and ensure consistent assessment standards. Sometimes such independence is realised through nationally or regionally organised examinations, including practical assessments, which are independent of local teachers and trainers. However, the assessment of variable real-world tasks necessarily involves local actors. Sometimes an independent assessment can usefully balance a local assessment. For example in Korea, technical qualifications are typically awarded after an internal assessment undertaken by a training institute, and an external assessment undertaken by the awarding body, with the award depending on an adequate score in both assessments.

The implications for Brazil

Assessments in the Brazilian VET system should balance different assessment methods. To support reliability, assessments should include some standardised elements, such as written or practical assessment tasks which are the same or very similar for all candidates. However, there is also a need to assess the performance of candidates undertaking realistic work tasks, or pursuing practical projects in the workplace. These tasks or projects should be carefully chosen so as to reflect a wide range of competences required for the occupation, including soft and meta- skills such as creativity and teamwork, as well as more narrowly defined occupational skills, so as to provide a broader assessment of occupational competence taken in the round. In longer programmes, partial assessments undertaken periodically in the course of a programme can play a very constructive role in providing feedback to students and teachers on learning progress, offering partial credit, as well as potentially feeding into a final assessment.

Full involvement of the productive sector, including employers and trade unions, enhances the quality of assessment and certification, and improves the credibility of certification. The productive sector should be involved fully both in the establishment of new curricula in the expanded VET system in Brazil and in updating existing curricula, as well as in the planning of assessment systems, as the productive sector has the most direct and up to date knowledge and experience of required competences. The sector might also be usefully involved in undertaking assessments of individual students, as this will add credibility to the consequent certification of occupational competence.

Brazil should include an independent element in assessment. Those most closely involved in a training programme, including vocational teachers and employers offering work placements, have direct knowledge of students and their capacities and have a useful input into assessment. This should be balanced by independent actors in assessment, who may be less likely to have biases because of any direct interest in the outcome, and who are in a stronger position to ensure consistent standards.

References

Brasil Ministério da Educação/Conselho Nacional de Educação (2021), *Resolução CNE/CP N°1 1/2021 - Define as Diretrizes Curriculares Nacionais Gerais para a Educação Profissional e Tecnológica*, https://www.in.gov.br/en/web/dou/-/resolucao-cne/cp-n-1-de-5-de-janeiro-de-2021-297767578 (accessed on 17 November 2021). [9]

da Silva, E. and F. Vaz (2020), *OS JOVENS QUE NÃO TRABALHAM E NÃO ESTUDAM NO CONTEXTO DA PANDEMIA DA COVID-19 NO BRASIL*, http://repositorio.ipea.gov.br/bitstream/11058/10414/1/bmt_70_jovens_que_nao.pdf. [3]

ECBO (2016), *VET in the Netherlands*, Cedefop, http://www.cedefop.europa.eu/files/4142_en.pdf. [18]

INEP (2021), *Censo Escolar 2020*. [11]

Itaú Educação e Trabalho (2021), *Planejamento Estratégico*. [14]

Kauer, M. (2015), *The status (quo) of VET in Brazil: An empirical study about its function, meaning and impingements from the perspective of former dual system apprentices*. [10]

Kis, V. (2020), "Improving evidence on VET: Comparative data and indicators", *OECD Social, Employment and Migration Working Papers*, No. 250, OECD Publishing, Paris, https://dx.doi.org/10.1787/d43dbf09-en. [4]

McCarthy, M. and P. Musset (2016), *A Skills beyond School Review of Peru*, OECD Reviews of Vocational Education and Training, OECD Publishing, Paris, https://dx.doi.org/10.1787/9789264265400-en. [15]

Norwegian Directorate for Education and Training (2011), *Etterutdanningsmateriell for Fag- Og Yrkesopplæring*, http://www.udir.no/Utvikling/Etterutdanningsmateriell_FY/ (accessed on 10 July 2020). [19]

OECD (2021), *Education in Brazil. An International Perspective*, OECD Publishing, Paris, https://doi.org/10.1787/60a667f7-en. [8]

OECD (2021), *Teachers and Leaders in Vocational Education and Training*, OECD Reviews of Vocational Education and Training, OECD Publishing, Paris, https://dx.doi.org/10.1787/59d4fbb1-en. [17]

OECD (2020), *Education at a Glance 2020: OECD Indicators*, OECD Publishing, Paris, https://doi.org/10.1787/69096873-en. [2]

OECD (2020), *OECD Economic Surveys: Brazil 2020*, OECD Publishing, Paris, https://dx.doi.org/10.1787/250240ad-en. [1]

OECD (2019), *Country Note Brazil. Education at a Glance 2019*, https://www.oecd.org/education/education-at-a-glance/EAG2019_CN_BRA.pdf (accessed on 26 November 2021). [7]

OECD (2017), *OECD Handbook for Internationally Comparative Education Statistics: Concepts, Standards, Definitions and Classifications*, OECD Publishing, Paris, https://dx.doi.org/10.1787/9789264279889-en. [5]

OECD (2014), *Investing in Youth: Brazil*, Investing in Youth, OECD Publishing, Paris, https://dx.doi.org/10.1787/9789264208988-en. [12]

Salas, P. (2021), "New High School: see how the implementation is in all state networks in the country", *Nova Escola*, https://novaescola.org.br/conteudo/20825/novo-ensino-medio-veja-como-esta-a-implementacao-em-todas-as-redes-estaduais-do-pais (accessed on 22 January 2022). [16]

Souza, A. et al. (2015), *Vocational Education and Training in Brazil. Knowledge Sharing Forum on Development Experiences: Comparative Experiences of Korea and Latin America and the Caribbean*, Inter-Development American Bank. [13]

UNESCO (2021), *Glossary. Out-of-school rate*, http://uis.unesco.org/en/glossary-term/out-school-rate-1-year-primary-primary-education-lower-secondary-education-upper. [6]

Note

[1] The breakdown of employment rates by upper secondary programme orientation (vocational versus general academic) is not available for Brazil in the OECD data.

2 Effective strategies for expanding vocational education and training in Brazil

This chapter discusses some of the key challenges and opportunities associated with the planned expansion of the Brazilian vocational education and training (VET) system. It looks at the different roles that VET can play and the diverse populations it can serve. The chapter also discusses the challenges schools may face to create new or expand existing VET programmes, and the support they might need to make the right choices. Lastly, the chapter zooms in on the need to invest in a skilled VET teacher workforce to support the growing number of students.

Making VET work for a diverse group of students

Vocational education and training (VET) serves different populations and aims to achieve a range of objectives depending on its target population. VET programmes may be designed to equip students with medium-level vocational skills and prepare them for entry into the labour market and/or to continue in education. Some programmes target higher-level skills and lead to postsecondary or tertiary qualifications. There are also programmes that focus on lower-level vocational skills and aim to provide job-relevant skills to those who dropped out from school or are at risk of dropping out (Kis, 2020[1]). These different purposes tend to be associated with different programme characteristics (e.g. duration, level) and student characteristics (e.g. age, full-time vs. part-time enrolment).

The intensity and depth of the occupational training in upper secondary VET can vary largely. In some countries, such as Switzerland, Germany and Hungary, VET is designed to prepare for entry into the labour market and involves substantial vocational training. In some other countries, such as the United States, VET in upper secondary schools is more about career exploration rather than full preparation for a job. In the United States occupational education and training takes place after the completion of upper secondary education through the network of community colleges, and lasts one or two years.

While in many countries vocational programmes do not enjoy the same status as academic programmes, often because academic selection means that vocational tracks may concentrate students with lower attainment, this is not the case in Brazil. There is much excess demand for many public vocational schools reflecting their elite status. In fact, many VET students in Brazil continue to higher education upon completion of upper secondary VET. However, it is uncertain how well these programmes prepare for the labour market, and whether academically demanding VET can cater to a wider population, and in particularly to those who are less academically oriented. Bearing in mind that the Brazilian VET reform aims to triple the number of students in VET programmes between 2014-2024, the student population in VET will certainly become more heterogeneous and VET programmes will have to adapt to address their different needs. Given the large number of young people who do not manage to complete upper secondary education in Brazil, there is also a need to reach out and train those who are at risk of dropping out.

For Brazil, the planned expansion of upper secondary VET based on the integrated model presents significant challenges. Similar challenges are found in Costa Rica, which shares some similarities with the VET arrangements found in Brazil and is also seeking to expand its VET system (see Box 2.1). The fundamental dilemma is how to prepare students *both* for further academic study, including higher education, *and* offering the kind of thorough training that will make an individual job-ready. The difficult choices involved include making programmes less academically demanding (as for example in dual system apprenticeships), extending the length of the programme (as in Latvia, Estonia and Costa Rica), and diversifying VET programmes in terms of their academic content. These strategic choices need to be addressed in Brazil. This section discusses these different options, how academic and vocational content are provided in other countries, and how VET provision can be diversified to fit students with different characteristics and learning preferences.

> **Box 2.1. Upper secondary VET in Costa Rica: Some lessons for Brazil?**
>
> Despite the huge differences in country size, Costa Rica and Brazil face some parallel challenges in upper secondary vocational education and training. Like the integrated model in Brazil, upper secondary VET in Costa Rica involves a demanding programme, followed by a small proportion of the youth cohort, leading to a double qualification and many of the students go on into higher education rather than into the labour market. Like Brazil, Costa Rica aims to dramatically expand participation in these vocational programmes.
>
> In Costa Rica, following comprehensive lower secondary education, students choose between two main tracks: academic or vocational from 10th grade onwards. In 2015, almost 72% of upper secondary school students were in the academic track, and 28% were in the vocational track. Both tracks lead to the *Bachillerato* exam and qualification, which is both a signal in the labour market and an important means of access to good public universities. The academic track offers 23 study alternatives and lasts two years, while the vocational track offers 7 agriculture, 24 industry and 25 service specialities and takes three years, with longer hours of study than the academic track, so as to accommodate vocational content as well as the academic content. Those who already have the *Bachillerato* may seek a vocational qualification through two years of night school.
>
> Between 2006 and 2014 the number of academic secondary schools increased by 11%, while the number of vocational schools increased by 52% between 2000 and 2016 (from 90 to 135), and there are ambitious plans for further expansion of vocational enrolments. Some 60% of those who graduate from the vocational schools continue in education, and the vocational school system plays a very small role in directly preparing young people for the labour market.
>
> At present, the technical vocational route involves a demanding programme of study that includes both the *Bachillerato* and an additional technical qualification. While this grants status to the technical schools, it leaves few options for those young people who by 10th grade may have become disenchanted by academic study, or who may have less academic ability, but who might be engaged by, and indeed excel in, more practical forms of learning. In response, the OECD recommended the concentration of high-level technical training in a set of specialised technical colleges, providing both upper secondary technical education, including the *Bachillerato*, and short post-secondary professional qualifications. Such specialised technical institutions would straddle the divide between upper secondary and post-secondary, allowing a relatively seamless transition for technical graduates into a short postsecondary programme in the same institution. Brazil might consider a similar approach, given the parallel circumstances.
>
> Source: OECD (2017[2]), *Education in Costa Rica, Reviews of National Policies for Education*, https://dx.doi.org/10.1787/9789264277335-en.

Different ways of combining academic and vocational content

Initial VET programmes in OECD countries traditionally have been designed for immediate labour market entry. In response to changing skill requirements of jobs and increasing demand for tertiary education from students and their parents, many countries have reformed their VET system to also provide a route into higher levels of education, including post-secondary programmes leading to high-paying jobs. Initial VET programmes that have not been reformed and offer weak routes of progression become unattractive to students and employers, see for example the discussion on shorter duration VET programmes in the Netherlands in Fazekas and Litjens (2014[3]). In Denmark, weak opportunities for transition from apprenticeship to post-secondary education have been suggested as one cause of falling participation in youth apprenticeship (Jørgensen, 2017[4]). In Brazil, upper secondary VET gives an eligibility to sit an entry test to higher education and enjoys high status. The challenge is to diversify VET provision to make it more accessible, with some programmes offering a 'lighter' academic preparation, without damaging the reputation of VET.

Many countries developed provision of post-secondary VET programmes that builds on upper secondary VET qualifications, and that allows completers of upper secondary VET to continue in education at a higher level. In Brazil, less than 10% of young adults enrolled in higher education pursue short post-secondary programmes, fewer than in other Latin American countries such as Columbia, Peru, Chile and Argentina (Ferreyra et al., 2021[5]). Brazil may consider further developing post-secondary VET options, so as to increase attractiveness of upper secondary VET and to boost the supply of skilled labour.

When VET students can continue to higher-level education they have to meet academic standards for entry to and success in higher-level institutions. Academic content (such as mathematics, language) that is required to successfully continue at higher-level programmes can either be integrated into VET programmes or be an optional add-on. Moreover, within VET provision some programmes may be academically more demanding than others, addressing the different needs and preference among the diverse VET student population.

Integrated VET and academic content

Some VET programmes integrate an academic and vocational assessment. This is the case for the French *baccalauréat professionnel*, for which the overall mark (out of 20) includes marks for academic subjects such as maths and French alongside marks awarded for demonstrating occupational competence during a placement (Field, 2021[6]). Completion of both vocational and academic qualifications, may require extra effort and time from students, as in fact students work towards a double qualification. To address falling attractiveness of traditional apprenticeships, Denmark has created a hybrid qualification (EUX) providing young people both with an apprenticeship and access to higher education. These programmes are academically demanding, and cater only to a few percent of those in the vocational track, but they have attracted some strong performers who would otherwise not have considered an apprenticeship. One potential risk identified by some commentators is that these combined programmes may turn into academic programmes with the vocational element being lost (Jørgensen, 2017[4]). In Poland, school-based upper secondary VET programmes ending with a final exam giving eligibility to higher education are one year longer than upper secondary academic programmes (Kuczera and Jeon, 2019[7]).

Add-on programmes

Alternatively, VET programmes may not automatically offer eligibility for higher education but VET students or graduates who would like to continue into higher level programmes have the option of taking additional academic courses on top of a vocational qualification. For example in Switzerland, students following the apprenticeship programme may opt to take additional courses leading to an examination that qualifies them for entry to some higher education institutions (in addition to their vocational qualification). In Sweden, academic courses giving eligibility to higher education are optional but available within VET programmes. Around 70% of VET students complete their upper secondary education with a diploma (Ministry of Education Sweden, 2018[8]; Statistics Sweden (SCB), 2017[9]), and out of those 41% become eligible for higher education (Ministry of Education Sweden, 2018[8]). To further improve access, since 2017, all adults have the right to study courses that give access to higher education in adult education. So, the option of higher education remains open for those who did not successfully complete their upper secondary programme or did not acquire eligibility for higher education. Box 2.2 below provides examples of add-on options linking VET programmes with higher education.

> ### Box 2.2. Bridging programmes linking VET with higher education
>
> In **Estonia**, upper secondary VET graduates who earn at least 60 credit points in general subjects can continue to higher education. They can then spend an additional year taking general education subjects to prepare better for higher education studies, or for state examinations which can be needed to enter some higher education institutions. However, the additional year option has not been used by many graduates.
>
> In **Colombia**, some vocational and technological institutes offer a preparatory cycle enabling students to progress to a higher-level programme, but in 2011 only 4% of university programmes could be accessed from such cycles. Consequently, very few students transition from vocational institutes to universities in Colombia.
>
> In **Indonesia**, entrance to polytechnic institutes is tied to entrance exams that rely mainly on academic skills, favouring general secondary school graduates rather than vocational graduates. In response, public polytechnics have taken measures to assess VET graduates based on their achievement at school.
>
> In **Latvia,** the shorter (two or three-year) upper secondary VET programmes need to be supplemented by one additional year of study to gain access to higher education through general education exams in Latvian, mathematics, a foreign language and one subject selected by the student. 15% of students pursued this bridging programme in 2013–14.
>
> In **Norway**, there are several points of entry to higher education. Among others, students in apprenticeship programmes can take additional academic courses while studying or a one-year bridging programme after completing their apprenticeship. In Norway, apprenticeship topped up with an extra year implies five years in total, as compared to the three years required to complete academic upper secondary programmes (Cedefop, 2013[10]).
>
> Source: Adapted from Field, S. and A. Guez (2018[11]), *Pathways of Progression: Between Technical and Vocational Education and Training and Post-Secondary Education*, http://unesdoc.unesco.org/images/0026/002659/265943e.pdf.

Diversified VET programmes with different academic requirements

VET can cater to a diverse population. In Switzerland, more than 70% of 15-year-olds with middle and low reading skills, and around 40% of high performers (as measured by PISA 2000), enter upper secondary vocational education (Meyer, 2003[12]). Likewise, in Sweden there is a lot of variation in students' performance across VET programmes (Skolverket, 2017[13]). In many countries students can obtain upper secondary vocational qualifications and opt out from obtaining an academic upper secondary diploma. In Brazil, vocational qualifications are only awarded to those who complete their academic upper secondary studies. This arrangement may leave less academically oriented students with no qualification if they do not complete successfully their upper secondary education. Inclusion of demanding academic content in all VET programmes can be detrimental to less academically oriented students and may contribute to higher drop-out rates in this population. Brazil may consider providing various VET programmes or tracks that cater to the needs of different target populations.

Differences in the target population can be reflected in the content and objectives of different programmes. VET should be attractive and challenging enough to those who favour more academic content and to those who prefer more applied and practice-oriented learning. To diversify provision some VET programmes can be more academically demanding than others. For example, in Switzerland, all apprentices receive 2.5 hours per week of teaching in the official language, communication, civic education (including some applied mathematics) and 45 minutes of physical education. This adds up to 120 hours of basic skills education and sport per year – so approaching 400 hours over a 3-year apprenticeship. But some programmes are more demanding: an apprenticeship in clock making (in addition to the mandatory 2.5 hours block) requires 90 minutes in mathematics and 45 minutes in informatics per week in the first year; 45 minutes in mathematics and 45 minutes in physics in the second year; and 45 minutes in physics in the third year (Kuczera and Field, 2018[14]).

Special forms of VET targeted at youth at risk

VET can also be an attractive option for less academically oriented students. Some countries offer VET programmes to students at risk of dropping out. Given a large number of students dropping out from upper secondary education and potentially untapped demand for more applied and less academic programmes in Brazil such shorter VET programmes targeting disadvantaged youth should be considered. While some students in Brazil exit education for financial reasons, some others may do so because they are not able to cope with learning requirements in regular programmes. This last category would particularly benefit from VET programmes targeting youth at risk.

These programmes are typically shorter than regular VET programmes, are provided as apprenticeship and target young people who are less academically oriented and are at risk of dropping out from mainstream education. In Norway, shorter two-year apprenticeships (*Praksisbrev*) are provided alongside regular apprenticeships (Norwegian Ministry of Education and Research, n.d.[15]). Similarly, Switzerland offers two-year 'EBA' apprenticeships (*Grundbildung mit Eidgenössischem Berufsattest*) designed for youth who face difficulties at school, struggle to find a three or four-year apprenticeship, or risk dropping out. The risk of providing VET to disengaged students is that VET programmes would be labelled as a pathway for dropout. VET programmes for youth at risk should not in any case be a dead-end, i.e. they should lead to a qualification that is recognised on the labour market and allow students who successfully complete this stage to continue seamlessly at a higher level VET programme. The programmes in Norway and Switzerland lead to qualifications that are recognised both on the labour market and within the education system, and allow graduates to continue into regular apprenticeship. Available evidence points to positive outcomes from these programmes. In Norway the programme has been scaled up after a positive evaluation of the pilot. In Switzerland nearly half of the programme completers proceed to higher-level apprenticeships, and among those who do not, 75% find a job upon completion (Kis, 2016[16]). The fact that these programmes end with a formal qualification is an important feature. (Kammermann, Stalder and Hättich (2011[17]) argue that two-year apprenticeships leading to a qualification are associated with better labour market outcomes than identical but uncertified programmes. In Switzerland in 2014, there were 5 900 students in two-year apprenticeship as compared to 61 000 in regular programmes (SERI, 2016[18]).

In academic education, there is a relatively well understood set of approaches designed to support those who struggle in the classroom. In strong school systems, those facing the greatest challenges receive extra coaching, formally or informally; mentoring is offered; wider personal or social problems affecting school performance are addressed. In some countries, apprentices may receive similar support when they face difficulties, designed to help them complete. This is often the responsibility of local authorities. For example, in Germany 'apprenticeship assistance', available to apprentice dropouts, supports transition into another apprenticeship or training programme. Assistance includes remedial education (language skills, theoretical and practical instruction) and support with homework and exams (see Box 2.3 for some further examples).

Box 2.3. Support services for apprentices at risk

In **Australia**, the Australian Government funds the Australian Apprenticeship Support Network (AASN) which aims to help employers recruit, train and retain apprentices. Seven AASN providers offer advice and support services for employers and apprentices. These services include:

- *Universal services:* the essential marketing, administrative, payment processing and stakeholder engagement functions required to underpin the Australian Apprenticeship. This includes an initial assessment of Australian Apprenticeship suitability.

- *Targeted services*:
    - *Gateway services*: pre-commencement advice to potential Australian Apprentices and potential employers of Australian Apprentices, in order to find the "right fit" and support employers to use apprenticeship pathways. Support includes testing the potential Australian Apprentices, recommending the right training or employment pathway and matching individuals with compatible employers.
    - *In-Training Support services*: tailored support to individuals assessed during Gateway Services or following sign-up as being at risk of non-completion. Support may include mentoring, mediation, extra support with study or advice and referral to appropriate services to address personal challenges such insecure accommodation, mental health, or financial concerns. This service will also support employers who need assistance with an Australian Apprentice they employ who is at risk of non-completion.

In **Austria**, integrative VET programmes (*Integrative Berufsausbildung*, IBA) target young people with special needs (two-thirds of participants), disabled youth and those without a school-leaving certificate. Training assistants, typically with experience with disadvantaged youth, provide specialist support to the young people involved. When IBA takes place at a training company, training assistants oversee administrative tasks, define the content of the training contract between the apprentice and the training company, prepare company employees for the arrival of the apprentice, and register the apprentice at the vocational school. Training assistants also act as mediators, provide tutorial support and design the final exam for the partial qualification pathway. When IBA takes place at a supra-company training centre, training assistance is provided by the centre's social workers.

In **Germany**, apprenticeship assistance (*Ausbildungsbegleitende Hilfen*) is available to young people taking an apprenticeship, as well as those who dropout, and supports the transition into another apprenticeship (or training programme). Assistance includes remedial education (language skills, theoretical and practical instruction) and support with homework and exams, which helps to overcome learning difficulties. Socio-pedagogical assistance (including mentoring) is also available, and this includes support with everyday problems and mediation with the training company, school trainers and family. The service is provided according to a support plan developed in partnership with the young person concerned. It is delivered through individual assistance at least three hours per week; there are also small group sessions. One particular aim is to reach out to youth with learning difficulties and those disengaged from school.

> In **Switzerland**, young people enrolled in two-year apprenticeships can receive individual coaching (*Fachkundige individuelle Begleitung*) designed to help them improve their academic, technical and social skills. Swiss cantons are responsible for implementation under a national framework and guidelines. Around half of the two-year apprentices take up this offer, mostly to tackle weak language skills, learning difficulties or psychological problems. Most coaches are former teachers (of vocational or special needs education), learning and speech therapists or social workers. They receive targeted training, which may vary across cantons. For example, in Zürich they must attend a 300-hour course and participate in regular team-coaching sessions. Apprentices may also attend remedial lessons at vocational schools, for example, in Vaud canton, apprentices may take time off during their work placement to attend school for remedial classes.
>
> Source: Kis, V. (2016[16]), "Work-based Learning for Youth at Risk: Getting Employers on Board", *OECD Education Working Papers*, No. 150, https://dx.doi.org/10.1787/5e122a91-en.

From an employer's point of view, taking on an apprentice with learning challenges will be a risk. But they may be more willing to take this risk if they know they will receive support during the apprenticeship to ensure completion. So one of the potential benefits of targeted support to apprentices at risk is not only that it will help completion, but also that it may help young people facing challenges to obtain a good quality apprenticeship in the first place.

Although evidence is patchy, studies suggest that support should help promote successful completion. An Australian study of apprenticeship completion found that many apprentices felt a lack of support and did not know who to contact for assistance, leading them to drop out. The interim evaluation of the Australian Apprenticeships Mentoring Package (Deloitte, 2012[19]) found that a credible party, independent of the employer and apprentice, can help address issues that may lead to dropout, such as problems in personal life, health issues and problems in the workplace. This issue has been addressed since, and in-training support services are part of apprenticeship contracts provided by the Australian Apprenticeship Support Network.

Finding VET teachers to support VET expansion

The attractiveness and quality of VET depends to a large extent on its teachers, and their capacity to teach occupation-relevant skills and to motivate and inspire young people. OECD (2021[20]) shows that many countries face acute VET teacher shortages. Ageing of the teacher population and the low attractiveness of the profession are some of the factors to blame. In Brazil, the reform expanding VET in schools will certainly increase the demand for teachers of VET subjects. Other country experience demonstrates that recruitment of qualified professionals can be challenging. This section provides examples of how other countries are addressing this issue that Brazil can draw on.

Recruitment of VET teachers can be difficult as VET teachers have to be acquainted with the area of specialisation (e.g. construction, electronics, hairdressing) and at the same time be able to effectively transfer their knowledge and skills to young people. VET teachers thus need two distinct competencies, specialist knowledge ideally supported with industry experience, and pedagogy. Requirement strategies for VET teachers vary across countries. Some countries require VET teachers to have gone through formal teacher training and demonstrate their industry knowledge and experience, whereas some others privilege one aspect over another. For example, in Austria, Finland, Norway and Slovenia, VET teachers should have relevant professional experience in the area they are teaching in addition to having gone through teacher training. However, in countries such as Korea and Japan, entry requirements are only related to qualifications and not to industry experience (OECD, 2021[20]).

Many countries have introduced flexible arrangements for qualified professionals so that they can teach in their area of expertise without too many entry barriers. These measures help address teacher shortages and ensure that those teaching VET subjects are abreast of recent development in the relevant industry. Obtaining a teaching qualification in full-time education may be too expensive or time-consuming for qualified professionals who in the course of their lives decide to embark on a teaching career. The cost of going through a full time programme is related to foregone earnings as participation in full-time education often cannot be combined with full-time employment, as well as the cost of the programme in countries where postsecondary education is not free. To facilitate entry to the VET teaching profession, many countries allow newcomers with industry background to complete teaching qualification while on the job or to shorten the training programme, see Box 2.4.

Box 2.4. Flexible VET teacher recruitment strategies

Korea

In Korea, teachers are civil servants and usually acquire teacher qualifications through examinations, but new measures aim to facilitate recruitment of industry professionals.

A fast-track teacher-training programme targets industrial experts in fields that have no established teacher-training course. This fast-track training will allow issuing teacher qualifications without going through an exam. It can also allow industry experts who are specialists in emerging technology, such as robotics or the Internet of Things – areas where there are currently no qualified VET teachers –, to be employed as "industry-academic adjunct teacher" while awarding them VET teacher certifications.

VET graduates who have worked more than three years in industry will be eligible to obtain VET teacher certifications. The country is also planning to allow VET schools more autonomy to hire qualified teachers based on labour-market needs.

United States

A recent law in Michigan allows non-certified individuals to teach in certain VET programmes as long as they meet certain requirements, such as having acquired 2 years of professional experience in the relevant subject area during the past 10 years.

Japan

In Japan, industry professionals with relevant experience may acquire a special or temporary teacher licence without going through the official exam if they have relevant skills and experience. Special part-time lecturers that can be recruited from industry, do not need a teacher licence.

Sweden

In Sweden, school teachers should be certified, but exceptions apply to VET teachers in areas of teacher shortages. VET schools have to ensure that these teachers have the necessary knowledge of school curricula and access to in-service training.

Denmark

VET teachers in Denmark are not required to have a pedagogical qualification prior to starting employment, but should begin the vocational pedagogical diploma education no more than one year after being hired and complete it within four years.

Source: OECD (2021[20]), *Teachers and Leaders in Vocational Education and Training*, OECD Reviews of Vocational Education and Training, https://dx.doi.org/10.1787/59d4fbb1-en.

In some countries it is also possible to combine a job in industry with some teaching responsibilities. For example, industry professionals may teach in the evening or weekends in an adult VET institution or teach full-time for a full semester. See Box 2.5 for an example from the Netherlands.

> ### Box 2.5. Part time arrangements for industry professionals in the Netherlands
>
> Hybrid teachers in the Netherlands are teachers who combine their teaching job with a job in another fields. It is estimated that there are around 50 000 such teachers. Several initiatives have been set up to encourage and facilitate hybrid teaching. For example, the Brainport Eindhoven region, in collaboration with various educational institutions and companies, has started a pilot to give technicians a taste of hybrid teaching for 4-8 hours a week. Windesheim University of Applied Sciences and ABN-AMRO conducted a similar pilot for bank employees in 2020. However, its use has been limited. According to a survey, general and VET upper secondary schools do not have human resources (HR) policies on hiring hybrid teachers (but it is "more a matter of coincidence"), which means there is no distinction between a teacher who chooses to work part time or a hybrid teacher who chooses to combine two jobs.
>
> Source: OECD (2021[20]), *Teachers and Leaders in Vocational Education and Training*, OECD Reviews of Vocational Education and Training, https://dx.doi.org/10.1787/59d4fbb1-en.

Supporting schools in offering relevant VET programmes

Schools may not always have the right incentives to offer relevant programmes

The Brazilian reform aims to expand provision of school-based VET and provide state schools with larger responsibility over the mix of programmes on offer and their content. But provision of VET may pose many challenges to schools, in particular to those with limited track record of VET provision.

VET programmes are more expensive than academic ones as workshop equipment can be costly. Cost differences between academic and vocational programmes are often reflected in the funding formula with VET students/programmes attracting higher funding. However, estimating the real cost of a VET programme can be complicated as the cost of provision differ largely across programmes, and if the funds are not earmarked schools may still privilege provision of less expensive programmes (e.g. programmes in business that can be provided in classrooms are less expensive than programmes requiring expensive workshop equipment such as programmes in aviation mechanics).

Workshop equipment should also be regularly updated to keep up with technological innovations adopted by firms, which may increase the cost of training considerably. Learning car mechanics on an old car can be instructive but does not prepare students for dealing with modern cars loaded with electronics. However, acquiring brand new cars for training can be expensive.

These are serious constraints and unless schools are supported, there is a risk they would provide programmes in areas that are easy to provide (e.g. in which they have equipment and VET teachers already available), but not necessarily in occupations for which the demand in the labour market is high. Moreover, schools may opt out all together from providing VET if they are given such a choice. Souza et al. (2015[21]) argue that the mismatch between VET provision and labour market demand for skills is already a challenge in Brazil as the choice of VET courses is decided mainly by VET institutions with little consideration for the labour market side.

Organisation of the school network and the choice of VET programmes on offer

VET providers may curtail the offer of expensive VET programmes and prefer to provide programmes that are cheaper to deliver, because they are more classroom-based or because they do not require expensive equipment. The cost of good quality provision is particularly high for small schools, where class sizes are small, or where unexpected fluctuations in student numbers mean that some teachers and workshops cannot be easily redeployed. For example, Swedish VET schools are very small, with average enrolments per VET school at around 100 pupils. Given economies of scale, the small size of schools increases the cost of VET provision and increases the risk that students will not be adequately linked to their career interest. Industry representatives in Sweden have expressed concern that some VET programmes are under-provided in some regions (Skolverket, 2015[22]). The French VET system is also characterised by a large number of institutions. In 2016, a VET school (*Lycée Professionel*) enrolled 300 students on average (Ministère de l'éducation nationale, 2017[23]). But a study by the Court of Auditors judged the system as inefficient. It recommended an increase in the size of institutions and a review of the funding mechanisms that currently favour small schools (Cour des Comptes, 2015[24]). Even in larger institutions the choice of vocational programmes on offer has cost implications. For example, provision of a wider range of programmes would typically be more expensive than provision of programmes in few selected areas. However, in remote areas with few upper secondary schools, a specialised VET institution may match student's interest less well than an institution with a variety of VET programmes. Countries address this issue by concentrating provision, sharing facilities and promoting school specialisation. An appropriate organisation of VET programmes can make them more student-friendly, for example by concentrating specialised VET coursework and WBL at the end of the programme.

Concentration of provision

By concentrating provision, the cost of providing VET programmes could be lowered and/or quality improved, as the fixed cost associated with running a VET programme, is, within reason, independent of the number of students. For example, if there are three schools in the area offering a similar VET programme, all three schools have to equip workshops and hire VET teachers to run the programme, sometimes in very small classes. Sharing the teachers and workshop either through collaboration between schools, or through actual school mergers, would therefore yield efficiencies. While there may also be economies of scale in general education, the need for equipment and a high level of specialisation mean that these economies of scale are more salient in the context of VET.

Economies of scale also apply to teaching staff, particularly in the occupational fields which are less common. Concentration of VET programmes in larger institutions may therefore alleviate VET teachers' shortages that may be expected to worsen in the future given the demographic trends in Brazil.

Larger VET schools could become regional VET hubs or centres of excellence, with high quality equipment and strong support of social partners. In school-based VET, schools often have to reach out to companies and are expected to establish collaboration with the social partners. If there are many VET schools in the region, and other institutions such as providers of courses for adults also seeking employers' involvement, such a large number of interlocutors makes it nearly impossible to establish meaningful collaboration of local firms with each school. Larger schools would mean that social partners' involvement could be focused more meaningfully on collaborative endeavours.

Many countries have concentrated their VET provision and promoted collaboration. In Estonia, Finland and Denmark a large share of VET students follow school-based VET, and all three countries have consolidated their VET provision, with a series of mergers leading to a considerable reduction in the number of institutions (see Box 2.6). The Netherlands is another example of country with consolidated VET provision, with many upper secondary VET schools enrolling several thousand pupils. These institutions have a capacity to address highly specialised technical areas with dedicated staff, and to purchase the very expensive equipment associated with these specialities. Many of these schools provide upper secondary academic programmes alongside VET provision. In the Netherlands, there are 43 regional multisectoral VET colleges (*regionale opleidingscentra*), 12 specialist trade colleges specific for a branch of industry (*vakscholen*), 11 agricultural training centres (*agrarische opleidingscentra*) and one school for people with disabilities in hearing, language and communication (Smulders, Cox and Westerhuis, 2016[25]).

Box 2.6. Consolidation of VET provision in Denmark, Finland and Estonia

Denmark

In a series of mergers have led to a considerable reduction in the number of VET institutions in Denmark. Remaining institutions are larger and can offer the student a greater choice of programmes. Currently in Denmark there are around 90 technical colleges offering upper secondary education. In addition to upper secondary VET programmes these institutions also offer higher technical and commercial examinations, programmes combining upper secondary academic and VET education and adult vocational courses. They can provide short-cycle higher education programmes and courses for enterprises in collaboration with higher education institutions (Andersen and Kruse, 2016[26]).

Finland

In Finland the majority of young VET students are enrolled in school-based programmes. In recent years the government has encouraged mergers of VET institutions. During the period 2005 – 2017 the number of vocational institutions decreased from 182 to 96, while enrolment only dropped by 2%, so that institution size increased dramatically. The 96 vocational institutions enrol on average more than thousand students (Statistics Finland, 2018[27]). In 2005 there were 60 institutions with less than 300 students, falling to 28 in 2013. A similar trend was observed in adult education, where the number of providers nearly halved between 2005-2017 (Koukku and Paronen, 2016[28]; Stenstrom and Virolainen, 2014[29]; Statistics Finland, 2018[27]). In parallel the Finnish government has strongly encouraged institutions and other stakeholders to co-operate and network.

Estonia

To increase the quality and efficiency of VET in Estonia, many small providers were merged into regional VET centres offering a wide range of qualifications. Adjustments will continue in line with demographic trends (Cedefop, 2017[30]).

Sharing facilities

Another way for VET providers to collaborate and achieve economies of scale is to share facilities. In South Carolina (United States) vocational courses are provided either on the upper secondary school site or in one of 39 training centres. Typically, training centres serve students from different schools in one local area, but 11 training centres cater to students from more than one local areas (Kuczera, 2011[31]).

Schools specialisation

In some countries, schools specialise in one or a limited number of areas (see Box 2.7 for an example from Sweden). Specialisation of schools, focusing provision on just one field, such as health care, has many advantages. One option is for students to start their upper secondary VET programme in their local school, with an emphasis on more general education and training, and then attend a more specialised VET school in their second or third year. This would require students spending a couple of weeks in a different location but would reduce the potential problems associated with younger students spending long hours on commuting, or having to live away from home during the whole programme.

> **Box 2.7. Branch schools in Sweden**
>
> In 2018, a pilot exercise was launched, designating nine schools in Sweden as 'branch' schools, offering specialised VET programmes in sectors and areas where provision is inadequate to meet labour market demand, either because there are not enough students applying for these programmes, or the cost of their provision is too high for regular VET schools. VET schools can apply for state grants to send their students for at least six weeks to a branch school participating in the pilot, obtaining the part of their education and training that cannot be provided in the local school. An advantage of this approach is that students can receive most of their education and training in local schools and attend the more remote institution only for more specialised education and training. The student's "home school" retains the responsibility for the student throughout the education, including for the education and training received at the branch school. The 'home school' signs an agreement with the branch school that states, among other things, how the student's education will be carried out and the amount of funding that the branch school will receive.
>
> The pilot will end in 2023 and if successful this initiative could be scaled up, with smaller and more costly specialisations concentrated in a small number of institutions.
>
> Source: Kuczera, M. and S. Jeon (2019[7]), *Vocational Education and Training in Sweden*, OECD Reviews of Vocational Education and Training, https://doi.org/10.1787/g2g9fac5-en; Skolverket (2021[32])), Offer vocational training through industry schools, https://www.skolverket.se/skolutveckling/anordna-och-administrera-utbildning/anordna-utbildning-pa-gymnasieniva/forsoksverksamhet-gymn/erbjud-yrkesutbildning-via-branschskolor (accessed on 26 November 2021).

Conclusions

The Brazilian reform aims to expand provision of school-based VET and provide state schools with larger responsibility over the mix of programmes on offer and their content. But the mismatch between VET provision and labour market demand for skills is a challenge in Brazil as the choice of VET courses is decided mainly by VET institutions with little consideration for the labour market side (Souza et al., 2015[21]). Brazil needs to consider how to support schools and co-ordinate provision of different VET programmes locally. Equitable access to high quality VET should be one of the criteria in the development of VET provision and school support. Otherwise, in a large and diversified country such as Brazil, there is a risk that benefits from the reform will not be distributed evenly, e.g. affluent regions will have high-quality VET provision whereas poorer areas will be left with no or lower-quality VET institutions. Moreover, the reform will certainly increase the demand for teachers of VET subjects. Flexible recruitment of skilled employees is one of the solutions to avoid teacher shortages and ensure that VET teachers have up-to-date industry-relevant skills and knowledge. This solution has already been introduced in Brazil as schools can hire professionals with relevant work experience but without teacher training (OECD, 2021[33]). This is in line with practices encountered in many countries. However, countries that have flexible arrangements for VET teachers typically expect VET teachers without pedagogical training to complete teacher training while on the job.

Brazil may consider providing various VET programmes or tracks that cater to the needs of different target populations. In Brazil, vocational qualifications are only awarded to those who complete their academic upper secondary studies. This arrangement may leave less academically oriented students with no qualification if they do not successfully complete their upper secondary education. Inclusion of demanding academic content in all VET programmes can be detrimental to less academically oriented students and may contribute to higher dropout rates.

References

Andersen, O. and K. Kruse (2016), "Vocational education and training in Europe – Denmark.", *Cedefop ReferNet VET in Europe reports;*, http://www.cedefop.europa.eu/en/publications-and-resources/country-reports/denmark-vet-europe-country-report-2016 (accessed on 16 July 2018). [26]

Cedefop (2017), *Vocational Education and Training in Estonia: Short Description*, Luxembourg Publications Office, Luxembourg, http://dx.doi.org/10.2801/15844. [30]

Cedefop (2013), *Spotlight on VET. Norway*, Publications Office of the European Union, Luxembourg, http://dx.doi.org/10.2801/50807. [10]

Cour des Comptes (2015), *Rapport public thématique sur le coût du lycée*, http://www.ccomptes.fr (accessed on 2 August 2018). [24]

Deloitte (2012), *Econometric Analysis of the Australian Apprenticeships Incentives Program*, https://www.australianapprenticeships.gov.au/sites/ausapps/files/publication-documents/econometricanalysisaaip.pdf. [19]

Fazekas, M. and I. Litjens (2014), *A Skills beyond School Review of the Netherlands*, OECD Reviews of Vocational Education and Training, OECD Publishing, Paris, https://doi.org/10.1787/9789264221840-en. [3]

Ferreyra, M. et al. (2021), *The Fast Track to New Skills. Short-Cycle Higher Education Programmes in Latin America and the Carribean*, World Bank Group, https://openknowledge.worldbank.org/bitstream/handle/10986/35598/9781464817069.pdf?sequence=4&isAllowed=y. [5]

Field, S. (2021), *A World Without Maps: Assessment in Technical Education: A Report to the Gatsby Foundation*, Gatsby Charitable Foundation, London, https://www.gatsby.org.uk/uploads/education/reports/pdf/assessment-in-technical-education-simon-field.pdf. [6]

Field, S. and A. Guez (2018), *Pathways of Progression: Between Technical and Vocational Education and Training and Post-Secondary Education*, UNESCO, Paris, http://unesdoc.unesco.org/images/0026/002659/265943e.pdf. [11]

Jørgensen, C. (2017), "From apprenticeships to higher vocational education in Denmark – building bridges while the gap is widening", *Journal of Vocational Education & Training*, Vol. 69/1, pp. 64-80, http://dx.doi.org/10.1080/13636820.2016.1275030. [4]

Kammermann, M., B. Stalder and A. Hättich (2011), "Two-year apprenticeships – a successful model of training?", *Journal of Vocational Education & Training*, Vol. 63/3, pp. 377-396, http://dx.doi.org/10.1080/13636820.2011.586130. [17]

Kis, V. (2020), "Improving evidence on VET: Comparative data and indicators", *OECD Social, Employment and Migration Working Papers*, No. 250, OECD Publishing, Paris, https://dx.doi.org/10.1787/d43dbf09-en. [1]

Kis, V. (2016), "Work-based Learning for Youth at Risk: Getting Employers on Board", *OECD Education Working Papers*, No. 150, OECD Publishing, Paris, https://dx.doi.org/10.1787/5e122a91-en. [16]

Koukku, A. and P. Paronen (2016), "Vocational Education and Training in Europe: Finland", *Cedefop ReferNet VET in Europe reports*, http://libserver.cedefop.europa.eu/vetelib/2016/2016_CR_FI.pdf (accessed on 11 June 2018). [28]

Kuczera, M. (2011), *OECD Reviews of Vocational Education and Training: A Learning for Jobs Review of the United States, South Carolina 2011*, OECD Reviews of Vocational Education and Training, OECD Publishing, Paris, https://dx.doi.org/10.1787/9789264114012-en. [31]

Kuczera, M. and S. Field (2018), *Apprenticeship in England, United Kingdom*, OECD Reviews of Vocational Education and Training, OECD Publishing, Paris, https://dx.doi.org/10.1787/9789264298507-en. [14]

Kuczera, M. and S. Jeon (2019), *Vocational Education and Training in Sweden*, OECD Reviews of Vocational Education and Training, OECD Publishing, Paris, https://doi.org/10.1787/g2g9fac5-en. [7]

Meyer, T. (2003), *When Being Smart Is Not Enough: Institutional and Social Access Barriers to Upper secondary Education and Their Consequences on Successful Labour Market Entry. The Case of Switzerland'*, Transitions in Youth Network (TIY) 2003 Conference., http://www.coreched.ch/publikationen/meyer.pdf. [12]

Ministère de l'éducation nationale (2017), *Repères et références statistiques sur les enseignements, la formation et la recherche*, http://cache.media.education.gouv.fr/file/2017/82/7/depp-rers-2017-etablissements-maj-dec-2017_861827.pdf (accessed on 1 August 2018). [23]

Ministry of Education Sweden (2018), "Review of VET in Sweden. Background report". [8]

Norwegian Ministry of Education and Research (n.d.), *Structure of Subjects in Initial VET*, http://www.oecd.org/edu/school/45158199.pdf. [15]

OECD (2021), *Education in Brazil. An International Perspective*, OECD Publishing, Paris, https://doi.org/10.1787/60a667f7-en. [33]

OECD (2021), *Teachers and Leaders in Vocational Education and Training*, OECD Reviews of Vocational Education and Training, OECD Publishing, Paris, https://dx.doi.org/10.1787/59d4fbb1-en. [20]

OECD (2017), *Education in Costa Rica*, Reviews of National Policies for Education, OECD Publishing, Paris, https://dx.doi.org/10.1787/9789264277335-en. [2]

SERI (2016), *Vocational and Professional Education and Training in Switzerland: Facts and Figures*, State Secretariat for Education, Research and Innovation. [18]

Skolverket (2021), *Offer vocational training through industry schools*, https://www.skolverket.se/skolutveckling/anordna-och-administrera-utbildning/anordna-utbildning-pa-gymnasieniva/forsoksverksamhet-gymn/erbjud-yrkesutbildning-via-branschskolor (accessed on 26 November 2021). [32]

Skolverket (2017), *Recognition of the mission on monitoring of the secondary school in 2017 No. 2016: 01706*, http://www.skolverket.se (accessed on 18 July 2018). [13]

Skolverket (2015), *An Assessment of the Situation in the Swedish School System 2015*, Skolverket, Stockholm, https://www.skolverket.se/om-skolverket/andra-sprak/in-english/publication/2.5845?_xurl_=http%3A%2F%2Fwww5.skolverket.se%2Fwtpub%2Fws%2Fskolbok%2Fwpubext%2Ftrycksak%2FBlob%2Fpdf3551.pdf%3Fk%3D3551 (accessed on 4 June 2018). [22]

Smulders, H., A. Cox and A. Westerhuis (2016), *Netherlands: VET in Europe: country report 2016*, http://libserver.cedefop.europa.eu/vetelib/2016/2016_CR_NL.pdf (accessed on 15 June 2018). [25]

Souza, A. et al. (2015), *Vocational Education and Training in Brazil. Knowledge Sharing Forum on Development Experiences: Comparative Experiences of Korea and Latin America and the Caribbean*, Inter-Development American Bank. [21]

Statistics Finland (2018), *Providers of education and educational institutions 2017*, http://www.stat.fi/til/kjarj/2017/kjarj_2017_2018-02-13_tie_001_en.html (accessed on 22 June 2018). [27]

Statistics Sweden (SCB) (2017), *Minskat intresse för gymnasiets yrkesprogram*, https://www.scb.se/hitta-statistik/artiklar/2017/Minskat-intresse-for-gymnasiets-yrkesprogram/ (accessed on 27 August 2018). [9]

Stenstrom, M. and M. Virolainen (2014), *The current state and challenges of vocational education and training in Finland | VOCEDplus, the international tertiary education and research database*, http://www.voced.edu.au/content/ngv%3A66853. [29]

3 Involvement of employers in the provision of training

This chapter looks at benefits of work-based learning as part of vocational education and training (VET) programmes and how Brazil can increase provision of work placements provided by employers to students. One of the main challenges in increasing work placement opportunities is that some employers may not feel able to train students. The chapter discusses various measures that can enhance the training capacity of firms, such as training of trainers in companies and facilitating collaboration across companies in the provision of training. Recognising the role of schools in reaching out to employers, the chapter provides examples of how the responsibility for work-based learning can be shared between schools and employers.

Making the most of work-based learning

In most countries, schools share the responsibility for training with companies, i.e. some vocational education and training (VET) is provided in schools and some by companies. Work-based learning (WBL) or work placement refers to learning through participation in, and/or observation of work, under the supervision of an employer. Vocational programmes including WBL typically lead to a recognised qualification, and involve a work placement with an employer that leads to the development of new skills. In programmes with longer periods of WBL students typically contribute with some productive work, whereas the amount of productive work performed by students in shorter WBL is limited. In Brazil, few VET students receive training in companies (see Chapter 1).

Learning in a workplace is an essential part of VET and yields benefits to students and employers. The benefits depend on both the length and quality of work placements and together these factors define how effective WBL is in developing the skills required in target jobs, and in transitioning people, particularly young people, into the labour market.

Workplaces provide a strong learning environment. WBL allows students to acquire practical skills on up-to-date equipment and under the supervision of trainers who are familiar with the most recent working methods and technologies. Rapidly changing technologies mean that equipment quickly becomes obsolete, and VET schools are sometimes unable to afford modern equipment. Workplace training will therefore often be more cost-effective, since it makes use of equipment already available in enterprises. In the workplace, students also develop key soft skills, such as dealing with customers, work discipline, teamwork, and problem-solving. Evidence indicates the growing labour market importance of soft skills (Deming and Kahn, 2017[1]) and suggests that many soft skills are more effectively learnt in workplaces than in classrooms (OECD, 2010[2]). Soft skills may be particularly lacking among disadvantaged youth, VET programmes may therefore facilitate the transition of disadvantaged young people from school to the labour market and boost their career options.

There is evidence that VET graduates who have experienced more WBL (such as apprentices) have stronger labour market outcomes, in terms of duration of job search, unemployment spells and wages, than those who choose another type of upper secondary education (van der Klaauw, van Vuuren and Berkhout, 2004[3]). Evidence from European countries show that young people with an upper secondary VET qualification who gained work experience during their studies have higher employment rates than those without workplace exposure (OECD, 2020[4]). Overall, countries with a high share of youth in apprenticeships have lower rates of disconnected youth and youth experiencing a difficult transition to employment (Quintini and Manfredi, 2009[5]). This is important, as first labour market experiences have lasting consequences. Youth unemployment has long-term scarring effects with high costs for both individuals and society (Bell and Blanchflower, 2011[6]; Nilsen and Reiso, 2011[7]). However, evidence on long-term effects is more mixed. Some research studies argue that while vocational education and training leads, in the short term, to positive outcomes by facilitating labour market entry, this initial advantage disappears in the long term (Hanushek, Woessmann and Zhang, 2011[8]). Forster, Bol and van de Werfhorst (2016[9]) confirm that VET is associated with early career benefits, with the benefits being the largest in countries with strong apprenticeship systems. They show that only in some countries, the early career advantage associated with VET turns into a disadvantage later on. In others there is no clear evidence of a negative effect. Benefits associated with VET therefore depend on the content and organisation of the programme. The results of the studies discussed above should be treated with caution as they suffer from many limitations. They draw conclusions based on an analysis of cross-sectional data, which means that they were unable to separate the age, period, and cohort effects that all influence career trajectories. A more fundamental underlying difficulty is that academic and VET programmes often prepare for different careers (Kuczera, 2017[10]).

WBL is beneficial also to employers. WBL yields useful work for the employer, and is a means of recruitment. When students undertake useful work, it benefits the employer (Kuczera, 2017[10]; Walther,

Schweri and Wolter, 2005[11]; Mühlemann, 2016[12]). Longer-duration WBL allows employers to develop some firm-specific skills in their trainees/apprentices, as well as the broader but still occupation-specific skills that are formally required as part of the VET programme (e.g. the physics of electricity for electricians). Employers taking on apprentices or trainees can observe their performance during the work placement and recruit the best from among them. In Sweden, a study evaluating employer benefits shows that WBL of 20-40 weeks in total in school-based programmes lasting 3 years facilitates future recruitment and lowers its cost, and increases the skills and motivation of company staff, especially for those employees who supervise students (Höghielm, 2015[13]; Karlson and Persson, 2014[14]). Employers reported that students who carry out their traineeship in the third (last) year of the programme are more skilled and are therefore more productive than those in earlier parts of their programme (although benefits from the productive work of students are overall rather limited) (Karlson and Persson, 2014[14]).

WBL ensures VET provision matches labour market needs. Employer willingness to offer work-based learning is an indicator of their support for the associated vocational programme. Employers can influence the number and mix of places in VET through their willingness to offer workplace training. Even short work placements can serve to signal the skills needs of employers, while programmes which are more substantially reliant on WBL (including apprenticeships, but also vocational programmes with a large element of WBL) can also be more responsive to changing employer demand, as a substantial part of education and training is provided in the workplace. VET colleges and schools, on the contrary, may find it difficult to respond to rapidly changing demand, as new equipment is costly, teachers and trainers cannot be easily retrained, and programmes take some time to complete. As a result, in programmes dominated by school-based provision, with little or no WBL, the mix of provision may be biased towards the training that schools and colleges can easily provide, based on their existing equipment and teaching staff (as discussed in Chapter 2).

Lastly, the provision of training in workplaces can lower the cost of VET provision by schools and make the VET provision less dependent on schools' facilities. As discussed in the previous chapter, the planned rapid expansion of VET in Brazil will mean that schools will need to make substantial investments if they want to start providing or expand their current provision of VET programmes. WBL may make this easier and can also contribute to making the offer more relevant. Given these and other benefits of WBL, the planned expansion of VET in Brazil should be accompanied by an effort of making WBL a systematic part of VET programmes.

Designing effective work-based learning opportunities

The intensity of WBL differs strongly between types of VET programmes

Across countries, WBL ranges from short work experience opportunities, such as work shadowing, to programmes like apprenticeship that involve extensive training on employer premises. In some VET programmes, a mandatory WBL component represents an important element of the learning experience. Other VET programmes are more dependent on schools, with work-based learning being an optional and sometimes minor element. As shown in Chapter 1, in some countries, such as Switzerland, Latvia, Hungary, Germany and Denmark nearly all VET students are in programmes with a significant WBL element, while in Italy, Japan, Korea, Spain and Brazil, VET is provided mainly in schools. VET programmes with a large WBL element are generally referred to as apprenticeships, but can be found under many different names. Table 3.1 compares work-based learning in apprenticeship and school-based vocational programmes. Inevitably, it provides a simplified picture since VET programmes are very diverse.

Table 3.1. Comparison of WBL in apprenticeship and school-based programmes

	Apprenticeship	WBL in school-based VET
Is WBL mandatory?	- In most OECD countries WBL is mandatory (e.g. Denmark, Israel, Germany, Finland, Norway, Sweden, Switzerland, and the Netherlands). - In countries such as the United Kingdom and Australia, apprentices have to be employed but whether apprentices receive any training on-the-job in addition to their regular work is not always specified.	- Can be mandatory (e.g. Finland, the Netherlands, Sweden, Romania) - Or optional (e.g. Estonia, Korea)
What is its duration?	Apprentices spend most of their programme time in companies.	VET students spend most of their programme time in school
What is the status of participants?	- In many OECD countries, including Sweden, apprentices have a special apprentice contract. - In some countries such as Australia, England (UK), Canada apprentices are regular employees.	Typically participation in WBL does not involve any change in the status of VET students
Do participants receive a wage/allowance from the employer providing WBL?	-In the majority of OECD countries apprentices receive a wage. -in few countries such as Sweden employers are not obliged to pay a wage to apprentices	Most of the time VET students do not receive any compensation from the employer.
What is the role of social partners?	Often they have a decisive role on many aspects of the programme, and in particular on elements of work places.	Typically an advisory role.

Source: Kuczera, M. and S. Jeon (2019[15]), *Vocational Education and Training in Sweden*, https://doi.org/10.1787/g2g9fac5-en.

A pathway with extensive WBL can be offered alongside school-based VET programmes

Extensive work-based learning is at the core of apprenticeship programmes. Many countries offer apprenticeships alongside school-based VET. In Austria, Germany, Denmark, the Netherlands, Norway and Switzerland the apprenticeship systems enrol a large proportion of the cohort. By contrast, in Sweden and Finland, the school-based path enrols the majority of VET students, and a relatively small share of students are in apprenticeships. For example in Sweden, enrolment in apprenticeship stands at around 11% of upper secondary VET (Kuczera and Jeon, 2019[15]).

In Brazil, apprenticeships (*aprendizagens*) exist but are not provided within the initial upper secondary VET. The practical component can be done simultaneously, in the middle, or at the end of the classroom-based training. Apprentices receive a minimum wage (although firms can pay more), work up to six hours a day (eight hours for those who have completed fundamental education), and have a special work contract of up to two years (OECD, 2014[16]). However, the number of apprenticeships is low. In 2012, there were only 260 000 apprentices (OECD, 2014[16]). While the reform aims to expand school-based VET, enriching the upper secondary VET offer with youth apprenticeships (as opposed to the adult apprenticeships which already exist in Brazil) would have many attractions. Some students may find applied forms of learning such as apprenticeships more engaging. VET expansion puts a lot of pressure on schools, many of which have limited experience with VET provision. Providing some VET programmes as apprenticeships would shift some responsibility for VET provision from schools to companies.

WBL typically represents at least 50% of the programme duration in apprenticeships, but the time-sequencing of on- and off-the-job education and training varies between different apprenticeship systems – sometimes involving one or two days a week in school or college as in most dual system apprenticeships, but sometimes in larger time chunks for the off-the-job component, for example in and Ireland. While some flexibility is often possible, the time sequencing of WBL is typically defined for apprenticeship programmes within the country. For example, in Norway most apprenticeships involve two years in school followed by two years in a company. This defined national pattern is very different from Sweden, where delivery of WBL is individually negotiated by the school.

Different populations or industries may prefer school-based VET over apprenticeship or vice versa: in the Netherlands, the school-based option is more popular with younger students, in sectors without an apprenticeship tradition, and in programmes leading to higher-level qualifications (ECBO, 2014[17]).

In Finland, vocational programmes in schools with shorter work placements are more popular among young people, while apprenticeships more often serve older students with some work experience (Stenstrom and Virolainen, 2014[18]). In Finland and the Netherlands students select themselves into different paths and a young person is free to choose an apprenticeship, and indeed some do so.

In some countries, different VET paths can lead to the same qualification. For example, in Sweden an upper secondary VET qualification in construction can be acquired through school-based VET for youth, through a youth apprenticeship or through adult VET. Other countries maintain similar arrangements. In the Netherlands, there are two vocational routes at upper secondary level leading to the same qualification: apprenticeships with on-the-job learning representing at least 60% of the programme duration, and school-based vocational programmes with mandatory work placements representing at least 20% of the programme duration (Smulders, Cox and Westerhuis, 2016[19]). Finland and Estonia also offer school-based VET and apprenticeship programmes leading to the same qualifications.

In some countries WBL in school-based VET is mandatory

Many countries recognise the value of WBL and make it a mandatory part of school based VET programmes (without the WBL component being as extensive as in apprenticeship programmes). For example, in Finland a work placement of at least six months is mandatory in upper secondary vocational programmes, and represents about 20% of the programme duration. The recent reform of the Finnish VET system further increased the role of learning in workplace. In the Netherlands, students in school-based VET have to spend at least 20% of their time in work placement with companies, with the average being 30% (Smulders, Cox and Westerhuis, 2016[19]). In Sweden, students in VET programmes lasting 3 years spent at least 15 weeks in work placements. But sometimes in school-based VET, work placements are optional. Israel, for example, has recently introduced an element of work experience in school-based VET that provides some students with the opportunity of observing real work during visits to workplaces, but the majority of VET students follow entirely school-based education (Kuczera, Bastianić and Field, 2018[20]).

WBL in school-based VET can be organised in different ways.

Arrangements for sequencing work placements are diverse. Work placements often take place in the middle of a school programme, and sometimes over a summer (when there is a natural break in a school-based programme). In other cases they are broken into multiple shorter periods of placement scattered throughout the programme, and sometimes right at the end of the programme. They may also be on a weekly basis, e.g. one half day a week. A number of competing objectives bear on the pattern. The arrangements need to be workable for employers. They may, for example, find it helpful to have extra pairs of hands at particularly busy times of the year. Work placements at the end of a vocational programme may allow employers to seamlessly retain, as full employees, the trainees that they prefer. Employers may also prefer to offer training at the end of the programme as students who are about the complete their VET studies are likely to be more mature and knowledgeable than students who just started on the programme.

WBL needs to be built into the vocational programme so as to be coherent with other parts of the programme. In Chile, for example, graduates of four year upper secondary VET have to spend the final four months of their programme in a work placement to obtain their VET certificate. But this placement is not integrated into the curriculum, quality assurance is patchy, and about half of the students do not complete their workplace training (Kis and Field, 2008[21]). WBL arrangements need also to be practical in terms of transport – it may be feasible to spend a few months with an employer in another part of the country, but not to travel there on a weekly basis. Box 3.1 sets out the arrangements in France.

Box 3.1. WBL in vocational programmes in France

Students preparing the professional upper secondary leaving certificate (*baccalauréat professionnel*), follow a three year programme that is predominantly school-based but must include 22 weeks of WBL. Students can participate in up to six work placements with each placement being a minimum of three weeks. There is a strong focus on integrating school-based learning within the job training periods. For instance, the qualification standards define which competences are to be acquired through the on-the-job training. Finding an employer for the student is the responsibility of the VET provider, and VET teachers have to identify and co-operate with companies that are most suitable to host their students. Students sign a training agreement (*convention de stage*) with the school and the employer, covering working time, health and safety or insurance but also the pedagogical aspects. Use of such documentation enables learners to observe, interact and reflect on what they have learnt and on the activities carried out during the training period. In addition, employers have a key role to play in the preparation phase before the training commences. Teaching staff together with employers define the practical aspects of the training period and determine the tasks the learner is required to carry out. To ensure learners are appropriately supported, support is provided by qualified mentors (Field, 2018[22]; European Commission, 2013[23]).

Source: European Commission (2013[23]), Work-based Learning in Europe: Practices and Policy Pointers. http://ec.europa.eu/dgs/education_culture/repository/education/policy/vocational-policy/doc/alliance/work-based-learning-in-europe_en.pdf; Field, S. (2018[22]), *The Missing Middle: Higher Technical Education in England. A Report to the Gatsby Foundation*, https://www.gatsby.org.uk/uploads/education/the-missing-middle-higher-technical-education-in-england.pdf.

Local partnerships are important to facilitate WBL

Often, the biggest challenge in the development of WBL is how to make it happen on the ground. The aspiration is to realise high quality WBL, fully engaging employers, delivered by well-prepared supervisors in supportive workplace environments, backed by an infrastructure of support from the schools, effective integration of WBL into a school-based programme, and a strong assessment framework. But bringing this aspiration to fruition is hugely challenging, particularly when implementation takes place against a background of weak employer engagement as a point of departure. One recent initiative to develop quality WBL in Latvia is described in Box 3.2.

Box 3.2. Development of WBL in school-based VET in Latvia

VET provision in Latvia is largely school-based, but since 2012, attempts have been made to develop and strengthen WBL as part of a broader VET reform that also sought to enhance the engagement of social partners. Reform efforts were guided by intensive consultations, championed by the Ministry of Education, and resulted in small-scale pilot interventions that applied a bottom-up approach in terms of design. Subsequently, based on the results of the three-year pilot, the WBL regulatory framework was adapted to allow for a further expansion of WBL provision. The implementation of WBL under the new framework started in 2016. Key elements are:

- A high priority given to WBL by national authorities (Ministry of Education and Science).
- A strong focus on stakeholder consultations, resulting in a shared vision and strong ownership of the reforms.
- A bottom-up pilot initiative preceded and informed the adaptation of the regulatory framework.

> The reform was informed by international practices, particularly through strong co-operation with stakeholders from countries with well-established WBL mechanisms, such as Germany and Switzerland Extensive and focused use of EU financing (particularly from the European Social Fund) will support the implementation of the WBL reform from 2016 to 2023, and is expected to contribute to the participation of 11 000 students in WBL activities (Hoftijzer, Stronkowski and Rozenbaum, 2018[24]).
>
> Source: Adapted from Hoftijzer, M., P. Stronkowski, and J. Rozenbaum. (2018[24]). Getting Out of School and into the Workplace: Strengthening Work-Based Learning in Upper Secondary Technical Education in Poland's Świętokrzyskie Region. International Development in Focus, http://dx.doi.org/10.1596/978-1-4648-1322-1.

One key precondition of effective WBL is local partnership between VET providers and the employers that provide the WBL. Such partnerships facilitate the initial offer of work placements, and the subsequent exchanges between VET providers and training employers that sustain the work placements and ensure that the placements fit effectively into the vocational programme.

In Australia, local industry-school partnerships have been increasingly recognised as a means of preparing students for employment (Flynn, Pillay and Watters, 2014[25]). Sometimes such partnerships may be underpinned by local arrangements which adapt the curricula in VET schools to the particular requirements of local employers. Likewise in Romania, within the frame of a nationally determined vocational qualification in the post-high schools, 15% of the curriculum is agreed locally in consultation with the social partners, subject to endorsement by the school inspectorate (Musset, 2014[26]).

Ideally, the responsibility for WBL should be shared between the school and social partners and their roles clearly defined. Looking at other countries, schools are responsible for education and training taking place on school premises, and often they share the responsibility for work placement with the company. For example, the school and the firm agree on the timing of WBL and the skills students should develop while with the company. In Sweden, local partnerships are set up by the school and often this responsibility falls on VET teachers. The VET teachers play an active role in finding companies that can provide work placement, are responsible for following the progress and development of the students at the workplace, and ensuring the apprenticeship agreement signed between the school, the workplace and the apprentice is observed by all the parties. However, reliance on individual teachers resulted in large variation in the quality of work-based learning in Sweden (Kuczera and Jeon, 2019[15]).

Individual VET schools may need support in developing their links with employers and their capacity to foster WBL. Sometimes this support may come from organised bodies, such as the SBB (the Foundation for Cooperation between Vocational Education, Training and the Labour Market) in the Netherlands (Box 3.4). It will often also be helpful for schools to find means to share their experiences. Systematic support for this form of sharing is provided in Finland in the shape of a manual, fostered by the Finnish National Board of Education (Box 3.3).

Depending on the place of the training different bodies evaluate the quality of training. Schools are evaluated by school inspectorates (or equivalent) while the social partners support the training provided by the employer. Social partners' tasks may involve certification of companies offering WBL according to agreed criteria and providing regular feedback to schools. Box 3.4 sets out how responsibilities for WBL are shared across different stakeholders in the Netherlands and the quality standards for companies providing WBL.

Box 3.3. Transferring innovative models of work-based learning in Finland

In August 2010, the Finnish National Board of Education with partners, published a manual for transferring innovative work-based learning practices, designed to help the many providers and stakeholders that are unsure of how to select the most appropriate model of WBL and how to transfer it to their context. The manual is targeted at a range of different audiences including VET providers, colleges, training centres and employers. The manual focuses on the process of transformation and innovation of VET programmes and WBL practices. The manual encourages VET providers to carry out a needs assessment, using measures such as a Strengths-Weaknesses-Opportunities-Threats (SWOT) analysis and peer review, to identify what needs improvement. It encourages providers to identify good practice among other providers by identifying those aspects that are not-context dependent and can be transferred. The manual also offers practical examples of how a VET school (as an illustration) can identify where improvements to WBL are required, how to plan to make such improvements and how to deal with changes that have been made (European Commission, 2013[23]).

Source: European Commission (2013[23]). Work-based Learning in Europe: Practices and Policy Pointers. http://ec.europa.eu/dgs/education_culture/repository/education/policy/vocational-policy/doc/alliance/work-based-learning-in-europe_en.pdf.

Box 3.4. Responsibility for WBL in the Netherlands: The role of bodies involving social partners

The Foundation for Cooperation between Vocational Education, Training and the Labour Market (SBB) (*Samenwerkingsorganisatie Beroepsonderwijs Bedrijfsleven*) in the Netherlands is organised in eight 'sector chambers' with social partners and representatives from the VET sector equally represented (ECBO, 2016[27]).

All companies offering work placements (both in apprenticeship and school-based programmes) have to be accredited and the accreditation has to be renewed every four years (ECBO, 2016[27]). One of the criteria for accreditation is the availability of a trained supervisor or tutor (*praktijkopleider*). Tutors must be qualified at least at the same level for which he/she is supervising work-based learning. Furthermore, tutors must be able to share their working expertise with students and be pedagogically competent (validated by diplomas/ certificates). In addition, the company has to offer sufficient training opportunities allowing students to develop the skills and competences prescribed in the curriculum. The company has to agree to co-operate with the VET school and workplace tutors have to contact the school on a regular basis. The work environment has to be safe for VET students.

SBB is responsible for maintaining the qualifications for secondary VET, for accreditation and coaching companies offering work placements, and collecting relevant labour market information. SBB also works on themes with a cross-regional and cross-sector focus (Smulders, Cox and Westerhuis, 2016[19])

VET schools co-ordinate workplace learning by developing or selecting workplace training course books, the planning of education and training offered in school, and facilitating sessions allowing students to reflect on their work experience. The school also keeps track of student progress by means of regular visits to the workplace ((ECBO, 2014[17]).

Source: Smulders, H., A. Cox and A. Westerhuis (2016[19]), *Netherlands: VET in Europe: Country Report 2016*, http://libserver.cedefop.europa.eu/vetelib/2016/2016_CR_NL.pdf.

Complements and alternatives to WBL exist

In addition to work-based learning in which VET students work in real workplace, various other strategies exist to have students develop practice-oriented skills in settings that are close to the workplace:

- Inter-company training centres: In some countries, they play an important role in delivering the curriculum in VET programmes. - they typically involve classroom-like settings for theoretical instruction and/or workshops for the development of practical skills. In practice, there are some differences across countries in how inter-company training centres are used. For example, in Germany, Norway and Switzerland they complement training in workplaces. They can be particularly helpful to support training in small and medium enterprises (SMEs) that often cannot provide a full range of skills to students. Students carrying out work placements with SMEs would receive some training in inter-company training centres. In Austria, they can complement training in workplaces or replace the work-based component for young people who cannot find a work placement (ideally, until they do find one). However, this arrangement is not optimal as students receiving their work placements uniquely in inter-company training centres do not reap the full benefits associated with work-based learning with an employer. Work placement in a training centre instead of a training with a firm can also be stigmatising. It sends a signal that the student was not able to secure a placement with a company.

- Dedicated workshops in firms: Some firms (especially larger ones) have dedicated workshops where they train apprentices before engaging them in the production process. Such arrangements are like school-based training workshops in that they are not part of productive work, but they are also like learning on-the-job as they enable students to learn from skilled workers in firms and using equipment in firms.

- Replicates of real workplaces in schools: These allow learners to reap some but not all of the benefits of work-based learning. For example in a restaurant run by a catering school, students cook and serve real customers, though they may not face the same pressures and expectations as in regular restaurants and they do not gain useful connections with potential employers. As above, replicates of real workplaces in schools targeting students who were unsuccessful in finding a work placement with a company may be perceived as a lower status option.

Supporting employers to engage in WBL

In Brazil, there are limited WBL opportunities in initial VET, but in programmes for adults, often run by social partners, WBL is more common. To develop WBL in initial VET Brazil may draw on experience of employers who already provide work placements to adult learners. Moreover, Brazil could learn from the experiences of countries with a well-developed WBL system. To inform Brazil on how other countries ensure the availability and quality of WBL, this section discusses various approaches helping employers to train. These approaches include financial incentives such as rewarding employers who train with additional funding or by making employers who do not train pay. Brazil has a long tradition of sectoral levy funds (related to Sistema S), whereby firms from the sector share the responsibility for training. It can be explored if training levy funds can be used to develop WBL in initial VET.

Employers' capacity to train can also be supported with measures other than financial ones. Provision of training requires additional efforts of the employer such as filling administrative duties, organising training on site, appointing and often training employees who are responsible for trainees. WBL can provide a unique and valuable learning experience to students but it is of little value if trainees are mainly allocated to unskilled tasks. Some unskilled work can be beneficial as it allows students to acquire soft skills, for example, understanding how to successfully complete an assigned task on time and how to become familiar with the work environment. However, students who undertake only unskilled work learn few new skills. To ensure that training in firms is beneficial to students, there are regulations defining the competencies that students should develop, how work based learning should be delivered, qualifications of VET teachers in schools and trainers of students in companies. The regulations and WBL standards are more important in programmes with longer periods of WBL as that is where students spend most of their time. While regulations ensure WBL develops in students the required skills, they may impose additional burden on employers and discourage them from offering training to students. Helping employers to meet various requirements and to 'teach' them how to train may be necessary to expand WBL opportunities in Brazil.

Capacity building and support measures

Some employers may not feel able to train students, and some are better than others at conducting on-the-job training. Training capacity depends on the quality of trainers, training methods and training equipment. It is typically less well developed in small companies that do not have dedicated training arrangements. Small companies may therefore particularly benefit from measures designed to enhance training capacity, such as training for trainers, assistance with administrative work and sharing responsibility for training.

Training of trainers

Governments can enhance the training capacity of firms through a wide range of tools. Trainers in companies are typically company employees who are responsible for training of students. They know a lot about the occupation and the firm but may know less about how to train young people. To ensure trainers have the capacity to convey knowledge and develop skills in students, some countries require or encourage trainers to take up an appropriate training. Governments may also facilitate networking among employers to share knowledge and experience on how best to support and develop students and put their skills to use. Box 3.5 provides examples of how training for in-company trainers is regulated or provided in various OECD countries.

> **Box 3.5. Training of in-company trainers**
>
> **Estonia**
>
> In Estonia, VET teachers are responsible for training of in-company trainers. They organise seminars and training courses, supervise and support in-company trainers. In the past, VET institutions could apply for additional funding to develop training of trainers. The purpose of the training is to raise the quality of supervision during work placement and the efficiency of such training. The course is between 8 to 40 academic hours long and participants receive a certificate. Training topics are about preparing, administering and evaluating work practice, and include for example didactics, supervision and training provision; curriculum objectives and assessment principles; work practice and supervision for special education needs students (Estonian Ministry of Education and Research, 2017[28])
>
> **Switzerland**
>
> In Switzerland, trainers at companies providing apprenticeships have to have a special qualification, that is awarded upon attending 100 hours of training in pedagogy, VET law, VET system knowledge, and problem solving methods for adolescents. VET trainers for intercompany courses have to complete 600 hours of pedagogy preparation and there are also special requirement for examiners (Hoeckel, Field and Grubb, 2009[29]). In addition to formal requirements, Switzerland provides in the QualiCarte a checklist of 28 quality criteria that are used by companies for self-assessment (OECD, 2010[2]).

> **Norway**
>
> The Norwegian Directorate for Education offers free resources for apprentice instructors on their website, including short movies showing how instruction can be carried in practice (Norwegian Directorate for Education and Training, 2011[30]).
>
> **England (United Kingdom)**
>
> Within the English context, a guide prepared by the Chartered Institute of Personnel and Development (CIPD) offers a range of advice to employers on best practice in mentoring and developing apprentices – but it is almost entirely voluntary (CIPD, 2021[31]).

Companies working together to provide training

To support employers that on their own would not be able to deliver WBL, many countries have arrangements that allow employers to share responsibility for it. Examples discussed below are mainly about apprenticeships but they can be easily transposed in the context of WBL of shorter duration. For example, in Denmark, small companies can jointly provide part or all of an apprenticeship (Poulsen and Eberhardt, 2016). In Germany "apprenticeship sharing" includes the following models (Poulsen and Eberhardt, 2016):

- Lead enterprise with partner enterprise model: the lead enterprise bears the overall responsibility for training, but parts of the training are conducted in various partner enterprises.
- "Training consortium" model: several small enterprises work together and take on trainees.
- "Training association" model: the individual enterprises establish an organisation for the purpose of the training that takes over the organisational tasks (contracts, etc.), while the master enterprises offer the training. The organs of the association are the general meeting and the honorary committee. A statute regulates rights and obligations of the members.

In Austria, companies that cannot fulfil certain standards (for instance because they are too small or too specialised to provide their apprentices with required training) may form training alliances (*Ausbildungsverbünde*) to share apprentices. Alliances of training firms are supervised at the state level by the Apprenticeship Offices (*Lehrlingsstellen*) appointed by Economic Chambers. The Economic Chambers help to find partners for firms willing to create new training alliances. Lachmayr and Dornmayr (2008) show that training alliances help to improve the quality of apprenticeship provision. In 2008, at least 5 000 training firms, or 15 000 apprentices, were organised in training alliances (estimation in Lachmayr and Dornmayr, 2008 based on Hoeckel, 2010). Group training organisations (GTOs) in Australia employ apprentices and hire them out to host employers, sometimes focusing on a particular industry or region. Their tasks include: selecting apprentices adapted to the needs of employers; arranging and monitoring training both on and-off-the job; taking care of administrative duties; and ensuring that apprentices receive a broad range of training experience, sometimes by rotating them to different firms.

Small companies may particularly benefit from these measures as they are less able to take advantage from the economies of scale that can reduce the unit cost of apprenticeship training. Such economies are realised when, for example, a trained instructor provides training to a few students at the same time, or the company bears the fixed cost of understanding the administrative and other requirements associated with apprenticeship. Small companies may also be unable to train for the full range of skills required by a specific qualification, which is particularly important in apprenticeships. Governments can support small employers, either through financial incentives targeted at small firms, or by setting up mechanisms that allow smaller employers to work together to gain some economies of scale in training provision.

Financial incentives

Financial incentives funded with general public expenditure: Tax breaks and subsidies

The provision of WBL can also be facilitated by reducing the associated financial burden on employers. Financial incentives for companies to offer training can be funded through general public expenditure, and therefore come from taxpayers, as: 1) a reduction in the tax base or tax due by companies providing apprenticeships; or 2) a subsidy to firms with apprentices. Existing incentives in OECD countries are mainly targeted at companies providing apprenticeships as they incur a much higher cost than companies providing shorter work placements for students. Some examples include:

- In Austria, tax incentives were abolished in 2008 and replaced by direct subsidies for apprenticeships. The Ministry of Economics and Labour considered the tax incentive scheme failed to target companies that would benefit most from additional support for apprenticeships (CEDEFOP, 2011[32]). Tax incentives have been replaced by a grant based system. The amount of grant received by the employer depends on the year of apprenticeship, with the subsidy decreasing with each year of apprenticeship (in the first year the employer receives an equivalent of three gross apprentice wages per apprentice, in the second year an equivalent of two gross apprentice wages, and in the third year an equivalent of one gross apprentice wage). Extra support is available to employers for the provision of additional training and for the training of instructors, and to employers whose apprentices excel on their final assessment or face learning difficulties. In addition, grants are available for apprenticeships that support the equal access of men and women to traditionally non-male and non-female professions (Federal Ministry of Science, 2014[33]) (Casey, 2013[34]).
- In France, all enterprises employing apprentices for at least one month can benefit from a tax credit. During the COVID-19 crisis additional exceptional subsidies have been given to employers recruiting a first-year apprentice. For large firms, these exceptional subsidies were conditional on hiring a certain number of apprentices.
- In Australia, employers that engage an apprentice or trainees can access a range of incentives through the Australian Apprenticeship Incentives Program. This includes wage subsidies of up to 50% of wages paid to apprentices and trainees during the COVID-19 pandemic, which aim to ensure workforce training continues during a period of considerable economic uncertainty.
- In the Netherlands, tax deductions were abolished in 2014 and replaced with subsidies (Casey, 2013[34]).

Financial incentives: Transfers from schools to companies

Provision of training in companies can reduce the cost of training delivered by schools, i.e. training that otherwise would be provided by schools takes place in companies. In recognition of the role of employers in education and training of young people, some countries transfer to employers providing WBL opportunities funds that would otherwise be channelled to schools. In Norway, upper secondary programmes provided in schools lasts three years, except for apprenticeship, where students spend the first two years in schools and the last two years in companies. Public authorities in Norway fund three years of upper secondary education. In the case of apprenticeship, it is the employer who receives one-third of the dedicated funding rather than the school. This model allocates resources from schools to firms without increasing the total cost of provision. It is thus a special type of subsidy based on the cost of VET student education.

In countries without a tradition of employer engagement in VET, schools play more active role in initiating and organising work placements and sometimes also in funding. In Estonia, the school designs a plan for apprenticeship study and may also design an individualised curriculum for the apprentice. In terms of funding, the school covers the training at school, supervisors' training and salary for the school supervisor. Based on the apprenticeship contract between the school, the company and the student, the school can transfer up to 50% of the cost of the study place to the enterprise to cover the salary cost of workplace supervisors (Estonian Ministry of Education and Research, 2017[28])

In Sweden, similarly to Estonia, only recently work-based learning has been promoted and expanded in upper secondary VET. Schools play an important role in arranging and supervising work placements with companies. Upper secondary schools providing apprenticeship can also apply for a state grant that is partly earmarked for the employer taking on apprentices. The amount of grant for employers is higher if trainers (company employees working with students) in the company have participated in the dedicated training programmes. The subsidy is therefore partially designed to promote training of company trainers (Ministry of Education and Research Sweden, 2018[35]).

Financial incentives: Training levy funds

Another option through which countries can encourage firms to set aside resources for training is by using training levies/funds, i.e. employers pay a (compulsory or voluntary) contribution to a pooled fund out of which training is financed. These levies or funds can either be mandated by law or imposed on certain sectors through collective agreements. Many OECD countries – especially in Europe – and some partner economies have training levies in place. For example, in the Danish and French levy system, all employers share the costs of apprenticeships. In Austria, Germany and Switzerland, levies are collected by sector; while in England, only large employers contribute. The size of employers' contributions varies significantly across countries, and sometimes even within countries when they are differentiated by sectors, firms size, or fund. Typically such a levy corresponds to a certain percentage of turnover or payroll (as is the case also in Brazil, see discussion below). Under levy schemes, funds from contributions may be used to support training in general and in VET for youth in particular. Training levies/funds can be designed in three different ways: i) revenue-generating schemes used to finance general training programmes; ii) levy-grant schemes returning funds to firms so that they can finance workers' training; and iii) levy-exemption schemes reducing the cost of training to zero when firms train, up to the amount of the tax liability (OECD, 2019[36]).

Levy training funds are often set up to correct for market failures, by supporting training that is in the collective interest of employers and society. For example, employers may not provide training because they fear that workers they train will be recruited by other employers. Employers benefit from a well-trained pool of potential recruits, and should therefore contribute to the cost of the training through a levy (rather than, or in addition to, contributions from general taxation). This point may apply to the training of current workforce and future recruits (Kuczera, Field and Windisch, 2016[37])). This last group includes:

- Young labour market entrants receiving initial vocational education and training in schools and sometimes in apprenticeships. Some labour market levies, particularly in Latin America are primarily focused on this group, and have been used to support initial vocational training systems.
- Adults in need of new skills, including the unemployed and those seeking career change. While the individuals concerned will benefit from the training, they can often not afford the full costs, and, on equity grounds and in the collective economic interest, their training should be funded.

Levy funds may also aim to reduce inequalities by targeting training of disadvantaged populations, or support small employers, including in the informal economy (Palmer, forthcoming[38]).

Levy training funds can span across all sectors at the national and regional level. They can also be set by employers up to address skills needs of a sector (or a few sectors). Employers have particular incentives to set up a sectoral levy fund when the cost of training is high, the labour market is tight and it is difficult to find skilled employees on the external market, and employers face a high risk that their fully trained employees will be poached by other employers.

Sectoral training funds are common in a number of European countries, including for example in Austria, Belgium (about 10 sectors), Denmark (10-15), Germany, Iceland (2-4), Italy (19), Luxembourg, Netherlands (about 100), Switzerland (multiple funds) and the United Kingdom (3). In Latin America, Brazil has nine sectoral training funds as part of its S-system, while Peru has two. South Africa has 21 sector training funds and is the only country in sub-Saharan Africa with this type of fund (the majority are national training funds). Sector training funds are also present in Australia (3 construction sector training funds in different regions of Australia) and Malaysia (Palmer, forthcoming[38]).

Brazil has well established sectoral levy funds that have been in place since 1940. Similarly to some other Latin American countries (INA in Costa Rica, INATEC in Nicaragua, SNPP in Paraguay, SENATI in Peru) sectoral associations established their own training facilities to train their workers and future recruits. Employer perception of the levy training funds in Brazil is positive. For example, employers consider that their employees educated by SENAC perform well at work; and 95% of Brazilian companies that hired people trained by SENAI were satisfied (Palmer, forthcoming[38]). SENAC and SENAI also conduct studies to evaluate the effect of training on employability of their graduates. More than 90% of SENAC graduates feel prepared to perform their activities after completing the course and 80% have improved their career options; 73% of people trained through SENAI found a job within one year of training completion (Palmer, forthcoming[38]). Given that the existing training levy funds seem to function relatively well, professional organisations running them should be included in the discussions on how to expand and fund provision of initial VET.

Overall, the effectivenss of a levy fund and employers's support of the fund depends on how it is designed, managed and evalued. Employers tend to be more sceptical of universal levy schemes, often perceived by employers as a tax (Palmer, forthcoming[38]; Müller and Behringer, 2012[39]). Levy training funds receive limited support from employers when the funds are diverted to purposes other than training, and when employers (and in some cases trade unions) have little control over how the money is spent. Palmer (forthcoming[38]) argues that some cross-subsidisation of non-levy payers can be beneficial (e.g. funding of training in small enterprises). However, too much cross-subsidisation may result in disengagement of the levy paying companies with the scheme. For example, levy payers may consider that their contribution is wasted if funds are diverted to low quality initial VET where the provision is driven by school capacity (available equipment and VET teachers) rather than employers' needs.

Challenges associated with financial incentives

As argued by (Palmer, forthcoming[38]) evidence on training levy funds is too scarce to draw conclusions on their effectiveness. Available evaluations on financial incentives for apprenticeships point to their modest impact on provision of apprenticeship training by employers. Westergaard and Rasmussen (1999[40]) found a significant positive effect of public subsidies in Danish firms, but only in manufacturing, office and retailing. In Austria, subsidies appear to have had a limited impact (Wacker, 2007[41]). In Switzerland (where there are no subsidies of this type), a simulation exercise suggested that subsidies would have an impact on firms not involved in apprenticeships, but would have no effect on the supply of apprenticeship training in firms that train already (Mühlemann, 2016[12]). An evaluation of the Australian scheme shows that the subsidy had only a small impact on the decision of employers to train. This was mainly because the subsidy covered only a small part of the company cost of offering an apprenticeship (Deloitte, 2012[42]). Another Australian study evaluates the impact of the withdrawal of a subsidy to employers, showing that it had no effect on employers using apprenticeships as a recruitment tool (Pfeifer, 2016[43]). However, the withdrawal of the subsidy led to a decline in apprenticeship provision in sectors where employers could not count on the long-term benefits of apprenticeships. These employers were not able to break even by the end of the programme without the subsidy. Muehlemann (2016[12]) argues that since in Australia the reduction in apprenticeships was particularly strong in the service sector, where the quality of apprenticeship provided was often low (as measured by graduation rates and employment outcomes), the subsidy may therefore have been promoting apprenticeships that were of limited value to individuals. The overall implication is that financial subsidies will typically involve a significant amount of "deadweight", i.e. training that employers would have funded anyway, even in the absence of the relevant incentive. Some element of deadweight is inevitable; usually the objective is to minimise its scale so that incentives increase the number of trainees. A further risk is that financial incentives may succeed in engaging employers who are primarily interested in the subsidy, rather than in training. Countries where employers have not been traditionally involved in training of students are more likely to subsidise employers providing work placements.

Large employers tend to benefit disproportionately from financial incentives (Müller and Behringer, 2012[39]). For employers to benefit from the subsidy they need to be informed about the scheme, e.g. on the existence of the measures, the criteria of eligibility, and procedures of application. Access to accurate and timely information may be easier for larger employers that often have training departments and staff dedicated to training issues. The provision of training and the use of subsidies also involve costs. The cost of these procedures may be less significant for bigger enterprises, relative to their overall training costs. Small enterprises may lack the capacity to determine training needs, plan accordingly and file applications for cost reimbursement or grants. It is therefore important to assist small companies with access to and the processing of available funding in parallel to providing financial incentives for training.

Conclusions

Expansion of VET in Brazil should be accompanied by an effort of making WBL a systematic part of VET programmes given the benefits associated with WBL. Provision of training in companies is more cost effective and can also contribute to making the VET offer more relevant to labour market needs. Helping employers to meet various requirements and to 'teach' them how to train students may be necessary to expand WBL opportunities in Brazil. Supporting the training of trainers and encouraging employers to work together are some of the solutions.

To develop WBL in initial VET, Brazil may draw on experience of employers who already provide work placements to adult learners. In Brazil, there are limited WBL opportunities in initial VET, but in programmes for adults, often run by social partners as part of Sistema S, WBL is more common. Brazil has well established sectoral training levy funds. It can be explored if and how this experience can be used to promote WBL in upper secondary VET.

References

Bell, D. and D. Blanchflower (2011), "Young people and the Great Recession", *Oxford Review of Economic Policy*, Vol. 27/2, pp. 241-267, http://dx.doi.org/10.1093/oxrep/grr011. [6]

Casey, P. (2013), *The Vocational Education and Training System in Netherlands*, UK Commission for Employment and Skills, https://www.gov.uk/government/uploads/system/uploads/attachment_data/file/303481/briefing-paper-vocational-education-system-netherlands.pdf. [34]

CEDEFOP (2011), *Using Tax Incentives to Promote Education and Training: Cedefop Panorama Series 2009*, Dictus Publishing, Saarbrücken, http://www.cedefop.europa.eu/fr/publications-and-resources/publications/5180. [32]

CIPD (2021), *Coaching and Mentoring*, https://www.cipd.co.uk/knowledge/fundamentals/people/development/coaching-mentoring-factsheet. [31]

Deloitte (2012), *Econometric Analysis of the Australian Apprenticeships Incentives Program*, https://www.australianapprenticeships.gov.au/sites/ausapps/files/publication-documents/econometricanalysisaaip.pdf. [42]

Deming, D. and L. Kahn (2017), "Skill Requirements Across Firms and Labor Markets: Evidence from Job Postings for Professionals", *NBER Working Paper Series*, No. 23328, NBER, http://www.nber.org/papers/w23328 (accessed on 8 November 2018). [1]

ECBO (2016), *VET in the Netherlands*, Cedefop, http://www.cedefop.europa.eu/files/4142_en.pdf. [27]

ECBO (2014), *Apprenticeship-type schemes and structured work-based learning programmes The Netherlands*, https://cumulus.cedefop.europa.eu/files/vetelib/2015/ReferNet_NL_2014_WBL.pdf. [17]

Estonian Ministry of Education and Research (2017), *Background Report for OECD on Vocational Education and Training*, http://www.hm.ee/sites/default/files/uuringud/oecd_vet_background.pdf. [28]

European Commission (2013), *Work-based Learning in Europe: Practices and Policy Pointers*, https://dual-t.com/contenidos/common/work-based-learning-in-europe.pdf. [23]

Federal Ministry of Science, R. (2014), *Apprenticeship. Dual Vocational Education and Training in Austria Modern Training with a Future*, http://www.bmwfw.gv.at/Berufsausbildung/LehrlingsUndBerufsausbildung/Documents/Die_Lehre_HP_engl.pdf. [33]

Field, S. (2018), *The Missing Middle: Higher Technical Education in England. A Report to the Gatsby Foundation*, Gatsby Charitable Foundation, London, https://www.gatsby.org.uk/uploads/education/the-missing-middle-higher-technical-education-in-england.pdf. [22]

Flynn, M., H. Pillay and J. Watters (2014), "Industry–school partnerships: boundary crossing to enable school to work transitions", *Journal of Education and Work*, Vol. 29/3, pp. 309-331, http://dx.doi.org/10.1080/13639080.2014.934789. [25]

Forster, A., T. Bol and H. van de Werfhorst (2016), "Vocational Education and Employment over the Life Cycle", *Sociological Science*, Vol. 3, pp. 473-494, http://dx.doi.org/10.15195/v3.a21. [9]

Hanushek, E., L. Woessmann and L. Zhang (2011), *General Education, Vocational Education, and Labor-Market Outcomes over the Life-Cycle*, http://www.nber.org/papers/w17504. [8]

Hoeckel, K., S. Field and W. Grubb (2009), *OECD Reviews of Vocational Education and Training: A Learning for Jobs Review of Switzerland 2009*, OECD Reviews of Vocational Education and Training, OECD Publishing, Paris, https://dx.doi.org/10.1787/9789264113985-en. [29]

Hoftijzer, M., P. Stronkowski and J. Rozenbaum (2018), *Getting Out of School and into the Workplace: Strengthening Work-Based Learning in Upper Secondary Technical Education in Poland's Swietokrzyskie Region*, Washington, DC: World Bank, http://dx.doi.org/10.1596/978-1-4648-1322-1. [24]

Höghielm, R. (2015), *Man lär så länge man har elever - Ratio*, Ratio, http://ratio.se/publikationer/man-lar-sa-lange-man-har-elever/ (accessed on 31 July 2018). [13]

Karlson, N. and K. Persson (2014), "Working paper No. 258: Effects of work-based learning on companies involved in VET education - Ratio", http://ratio.se/publikationer/working-paper-no-258-effects-of-work-based-learning-on-companies-involved-in-vet-education/ (accessed on 30 March 2018). [14]

Kis, V. and S. Field (2008), *Learning for Jobs. OECD Reviews of Vocational Educationa and Training. Chile: A First Report*, OECD Publishing, https://www.oecd.org/chile/44167258.pdf. [21]

Kuczera, M. (2017), *Striking the right balance. Cost and benefits of apprenticeship*, OECD Publishing, Paris, https://dx.doi.org/10.1787/19939019. [10]

Kuczera, M., T. Bastianić and S. Field (2018), *Apprenticeship and Vocational Education and Training in Israel*, OECD Reviews of Vocational Education and Training, OECD Publishing, Paris, https://dx.doi.org/10.1787/9789264302051-en. [20]

Kuczera, M., S. Field and H. Windisch (2016), *Building Skills for All: A Review of England, Policy Insights from the Survey of Adult Skills*, OECD Publishing, https://www.oecd.org/unitedkingdom/building-skills-for-all-review-of-england.pdf. [37]

Kuczera, M. and S. Jeon (2019), *Vocational Education and Training in Sweden*, OECD Reviews of Vocational Education and Training, OECD Publishing, Paris, https://doi.org/10.1787/g2g9fac5-en. [15]

Ministry of Education and Research Sweden (2018), "Skills beyond School OECD Review of Postsecondary Vocational Education and Training. Background Report from Sweden", https://www.oecd.org/education/skills-beyond-school/SkillsBeyondSchoolSwedishBackgroundReport.pdf. [35]

Mühlemann, S. (2016), "The Costs and Benfits of Work-Based Learning, OECD Working Paper" 143, https://doi.org/10.1787/5jlpl4s6g0zv-en. [12]

Müller, N. and F. Behringer (2012), *Subsidies and Levies as Policy Instruments to Encourage Employer-Provided Training*, http://www.oecd-ilibrary.org/content/workingpaper/5k97b083v1vb-en. [39]

Nilsen, Ø. and K. Reiso (2011), "Scarring Effects of Unemployment", *Institute of Labor Economics (IZA) Discussion Papers*, Vol. 6198, https://ideas.repec.org/p/iza/izadps/dp6198.html. [7]

Norwegian Directorate for Education and Training (2011), *Etterutdanningsmateriell for Fag- Og Yrkesopplæring*, http://www.udir.no/Utvikling/Etterutdanningsmateriell_FY/ (accessed on 10 July 2020). [30]

OECD (2020), *Education at a Glance 2020: OECD Indicators*, OECD Publishing, Paris. [4]

OECD (2019), *Getting Skills Right: Future-Ready Adult Learning Systems*, Getting Skills Right, OECD Publishing, Paris, https://dx.doi.org/10.1787/9789264311756-en. [36]

OECD (ed.) (2014), *A Skills beyond School, Commentary on Romania*, https://www.oecd.org/education/skills-beyond-school/ASkillsBeyondSchoolCommentaryOnRomania.pdf. [26]

OECD (2014), *Investing in Youth: Brazil*, Investing in Youth, OECD Publishing, Paris, https://dx.doi.org/10.1787/9789264208988-en. [16]

OECD (2010), *Learning for Jobs, OECD Reviews of Vocational Education and Training*, OECD Publishing, https://doi.org/10.1787/9789264087460-en. [2]

Palmer, R. (forthcoming), *Global Review of Training Funds*, UNESCO. [38]

Pfeifer, H. (2016), *Firms' motivation for training apprentices: an Australian–German comparison*, NCVER, https://www.ncver.edu.au/publications/publications/all-publications/firms-motivation-for-training-apprentices-an-australian-german-comparison. [43]

Quintini, G. and T. Manfredi (2009), "Going Separate Ways? School-to-Work Transitions in the United States and Europe", *OECD Social, Employment and Migration Working Papers*, No. 90, OECD Publishing, Paris, https://dx.doi.org/10.1787/221717700447. [5]

Smulders, H., A. Cox and A. Westerhuis (2016), *Netherlands: VET in Europe: country report 2016*, http://libserver.cedefop.europa.eu/vetelib/2016/2016_CR_NL.pdf (accessed on 15 June 2018). [19]

Stenstrom, M. and M. Virolainen (2014), *The current state and challenges of vocational education and training in Finland | VOCEDplus, the international tertiary education and research database*, http://www.voced.edu.au/content/ngv%3A66853. [18]

van der Klaauw, B., A. van Vuuren and P. Berkhout (2004), *Labor Market Prospects, Search Intensity and the Transition from College to Work*, https://ideas.repec.org/p/iza/izadps/dp1176.html. [3]

Wacker, K. (2007), *Teure neue Lehrstelle. Eine Untersuchung zur Effizienz des Blum- Bonus*, NÖ Arbeiterkammer, Vienna. [41]

Walther, B., J. Schweri and S. Wolter (2005), "Shall I train your apprentice?", *Education + Training*, Vol. 47/4/5, pp. 251-269, http://dx.doi.org/10.1108/00400910510601850. [11]

Westergaard, N. and A. Rasmussen (1999), *The Impact of Subsidies on Apprenticeship Training*, Centre for Labour Market and Social Research, Aarhus, http://old-hha.asb.dk/nat/nwnart1.pdf. [40]

4 Governance and framework for social partners' involvement in vocational education and training

This chapter focuses on measures that aim to reduce fragmentation and foster co-ordination in vocational education and training (VET) systems. Co-ordination of VET policies represents a challenge in many countries as different bodies and levels of governance can be responsible for VET. The chapter looks at how social partners, including employers and sometimes trade unions, can be involved at different levels where decisions about VET are taken, and provide their input on various aspects of VET.

Co-ordinating VET policies

A successful vocational education and training (VET) system needs strong individual vocational programmes. But such programmes, in isolation, are not enough. The vocational system also needs to be internally coherent, with clear relationships between different VET programmes and the wider education and training system, with clear routes of transfer and progression between vocational training and general education programmes. In addition, the vocational system needs to fit with wider social and economic requirements. This coherence and internal logic also needs to be transparent to all the stakeholders in the system. That will allow individuals to make informed choices, with an eye not only on immediate outcomes, but also on progress from one VET programme to another and into the labour market. It will also help employers to understand and relate to the different vocational programmes, which can increase their trust in the system and their willingness to engage in the design and delivery of VET.

The issue of co-ordination between various decision makers may potentially represent a challenge in Brazil as VET schools are run by a range of bodies including the federal government, states, municipalities, private providers from Sistema S, and other private providers (Itaú Educação e Trabalho, 2021[1]). Expansion of initial upper secondary VET would also require building a framework for social partners to advise on various aspects on VET policy.

In this report, the term 'social partners' designates both employers and trade unions, recognising that the composition of social partners differ by countries. In many countries, employees' representatives are involved in consultations about VET. Their point of view may differ from that of employers as they represent employees' interests. So for example, they may be in favour of a broader VET curriculum that provides individuals with strong general skills facilitating individual mobility on the labour market. Employers, on the other hand, may be more interested in provision of employer-specific skills that make individuals job-ready but which cannot be readily applied to another employer. The role of trade unions in the VET system depends very much on their organisation and their broader role in policy-making in individual countries.

Co-ordination across different levels of governance

The governance of VET is often complex, reflecting the fact that VET caters to different populations, such as young people in schools and adults returning to education, and spans across a range of sectors. Consequently, responsibility for VET can be spread across different bodies and levels of governance.

Different ministries can be vested with different responsibility for VET. For example, in Israel responsibility for most adult vocational education and training rests with the Ministry of Labour, responsibilities at upper secondary and post-secondary level are shared between the Ministry of Labour and the Ministry of Education. In addition, the Ministries of Health, Tourism, and Defence all have significant responsibilities regarding training in their respective sectors. Division of responsibilities can be a challenge if different provisions duplicate each other and are poorly connected. One effect of such fragmentation is that vocational programmes may be dead-ends, when students moving across programmes run by various ministries find it difficult to have their qualifications recognised and build on knowledge and experience acquired previously (Kuczera, Bastianić and Field, 2018[2]). Responsibility for VET can also be spread across different levels of governance, such as the national level, regions, municipalities and individual institutions. The exact distribution of responsibility depends on the administrative structure of the country. Typically, in countries with devolved administrations such as Germany, Spain, Switzerland, the United Kingdom and United States, sub-national units retain major responsibility for education.

Several strategies are used to reduce fragmentation in the VET system. Some countries do so by vesting one institution with overarching responsibility over VET. In Viet Nam, some parts of the VET system were managed by the Ministry of Education and Training, while others were supervised by the Ministry of Labour, Invalids and Social Affairs. Recognising challenges resulting from shared responsibility the legislation simplified the existing landscape and consolidated most responsibilities for the VET system under the Ministry of Labour, Invalids and Social Affairs (Kis, 2017[3]). In a federal context, a number of OECD countries balance decentralisation with strong federal institutions in the domain of vocational education and training. This is clearly visible for example in the federal management of the VET system in Switzerland, and in the co-ordination role of the Commonwealth government in Australia. On the other hand, Canada's Red Seal Program is managed by a voluntary intergovernmental partnership, which facilitates labour mobility and harmonization of apprenticeship training across provinces and territories through common standards and examinations. Co-ordination at the national level ensures that VET qualifications are recognised country-wide and VET graduates are employable in their field across the country. In Switzerland, the establishment of federal diplomas for the police and fire service workers (who are employed locally by the cantons) ensures that they can work in any canton (Fazekas and Field, 2013[4]). Some countries ensure that VET is provided efficiently by fostering collaboration between different bodies and levels, and sometimes create an independent body which role is to mediate and represent interests of various stakeholders (Box 4.1). Different measures are not exclusive, i.e. a country may vest one level of governance (e.g. federal authority) with more responsibilities and at the same time create independent bodies facilitating collaboration.

> ### Box 4.1. Bodies and mechanisms facilitating collaboration
>
> **Germany**
>
> In the Federal Republic of Germany responsibility for the education system is divided between the Federation and sub national units - the Länder. The Federal Ministry of Education and Research (*Bundesministerium für Bildung und Forschung*, BMBF) has overall responsibility for VET strategy. Individual qualifications are endorsed by specialised ministries (often the Federal Ministry for Economic Affairs and Technology), but need the agreement of the Federal Ministry of Education and Research (Hoeckel and Schwartz, 2010[5]).
>
> The Federation is also responsible for in-company vocational training, and the Ministries of Education and Cultural Affairs and the Länder are responsible for vocational education in schools. Ministries of Education and Cultural Affairs in the Länder organise, plan, manage and supervise the entire school system. They design the school curricula, train and pay the teachers and are responsible for legal supervision of the Chambers (*Rechtsaufsicht*). Due to this primary responsibility of the Länder there is substantial variation across states with regard to the organisation and content of teaching in the school part of the dual system.
>
> For vocational education and training within the dual system (apprenticeship), which takes place in cooperation between school and company, the Federation and the Länder agree on fundamental issues and in particular on training rules and regulations for the learning locations. To facilitate co-ordination between the federal government and Länder, a Coordinating Committee for Vocational Education and Training has been set up. This committee deals with issues relating to the co-ordination of in-company vocational training and vocational education in schools in recognised occupations requiring formal training (*anerkannte Ausbildungsberufe*) under Federal law (Standing Conference of the Ministers of Education and Cultural Affairs, 2018[6]).
>
> **The Netherlands**
>
> The Foundation for Cooperation on VET and the Labour Market (*Samenwerking Beroepsonderwijs Bedrijfsleven*, SBB) was created in in 2012 to facilitate interactions among different stakeholders involved in the VET. SBB involves all major players such as: the MBO Raad (association of all VET and adult education institutions), the AOB (largest teachers' union in the Netherlands), the NRTO (umbrella organisation for private education institutions), major lobbying organisations, employer associations, and major labour unions (SBB, 2021[7]; Renold et al., 2016[8]).

The SBB is organised into eight sectoral chambers responsible for workplace learning quality and keeping VET qualifications up to date in their own sector. Each chamber is supported by social partners. The SBB advises the Minister of Education on topics related to the VET such as skill needs, qualification and examination structures. It is also responsible for the accreditation of training firms and has a say in the design of the curriculum (SBB, 2021[7]).

Qualification files are the foundation of the Dutch VET curriculum as they set national education standards for all programmes. Each file describes competencies, skills, and knowledge provided and tested within each VET programme. The files also specify how each skills should be acquired (ECBO, 2016[9]).

Malaysia

Malaysia has a complex VET landscape, with programmes governed by 11 ministries and delivered in around 1 300 private, public and state government VET institutions. In an effort to bring more co-ordination into this scattered landscape, a national TVET Council (MTVET) was set up at the end of 2020.

The MTVET is the highest decision-making body related to the strategic direction of VET in Malaysia, and is responsible for improving the co-ordination in the system through public and private stakeholder involvement. The MTVET also serves as a platform for the government to empower VET in meeting the needs of the industry. Three strategic thrusts have been defined for this empowerment: integrated and co-ordinated governance, industry-driven VET, and VET shaping the future. These are supported by six key initiatives: formulating sustainable financing models; developing policies to encourage industry participation; creating a national VET branding plan; establishing a VET collaboration hub; establishing VET programme policies; and developing a one-stop VET data centre.

Good practice examples of stakeholder engagement already exist in Malaysia. A number of institutions have been successful in establishing direct links with business, such as the Penang Skills Development Centre (PSDC), which is dedicated to meet the immediate human resource needs of the business community and whose graduates exhibit an employability rate close to 100%. Similarly, Polytechnic and Community Colleges have regular engagement with industries through Industry Advisory Councils (IAC), and have developed work-based-learning and mobility programmes aimed at connecting lecturers and students with industry. (OECD, 2021[10])

Costa Rica

Costa Rica created the National Integrated System of Technical Education for Competitiveness (SINETEC) to co-ordinate and harmonise VET provided by different bodies. SINETEC was conceived as a body within MEP designed to integrate the different aspects of technical education. SINETEC is, on paper, composed of educational institutions both from the public and private sectors along with the social partners. Its objectives are: to co-ordinate the activity of training institutions and meet the needs of the productive sector; to promote technical education; to collaborate in the attraction of high-tech investment; and to advise the government in the field of technical education. However, some stakeholders have already suggested the revival of this institution as its impact is limited. The Costa Rica example shows that creation of a co-ordination institution is not enough. Institutions co-ordinating actions of various stakeholders should seek their active engagement and have a clearly defined role (Álvarez-Galván, 2015[11]).

Local autonomy

Co-ordination of VET policies should not eliminate local and school autonomy in some aspects of VET. Decentralisation may lead to positive outcomes by giving inspired individuals enough space for action and development of new ideas. It may foster an innovative and flexible approach, which adapts to the needs of local communities and individual employers, and in the public policy space, allows room for local innovation, entrepreneurial approaches and diverse voices in the debate. Local autonomy is particularly important in large and diverse countries such as Brazil, as it is highly unlikely that one set of rules and standards would suit all localities. For example, evidence shows that the ambitious programmes launched by the Brazilian government to retrain workers for employment in sectors with growing employment work best when they address local labour needs (OECD, 2020[12]). While these programmes mainly target adults, similar conclusions can be drawn in relation to programmes for young people (OECD, 2020[12]).

However, decentralisation typically results in a lot of variation if the outcomes are very much dependent on individuals. The objective is thus to ensure co-ordination of various provisions, typically organised at the national or regional level, while allowing some degree of innovation and flexibility at the local level. VET programmes typically aim to achieve objectives and follow standards defined at the national level. The national guidance and quality control ensures all VET schools in the country meet at least the required minimum. Ideally, national prerogatives are combined with local freedom whereby schools can often adapted the content to the local labour markets. Local freedom also allows institutions to go beyond the required minimum and set up strong partnerships with local employers. For example, in Norway schools in areas with economic activities related to petrol extractions, propose VET programmes preparing for the related jobs.

Systematically involving social partners

Why involvement of social partners is important

The vocational training system has to respond to the needs and interests of multiple stakeholders, employers in particular, as well as other labour market actors such as trade unions, so that training yields the right skills for employers, and supports individuals over a lifetime career. The engagement of social partners ensures that the skillsets embodied in vocational qualifications reflect occupational needs, and that the mix of training provision reflects the demand for jobs of different types. At the local level, good relationships between the vocational training system and social parents help to facilitate work placements for vocational students (see Chapter 3). Looked at across countries, VET systems therefore maintain a diverse range of bodies to maintain these links at national, regional and sectoral levels. At the national level, over-arching VET bodies engage the social partners, and typically serve the function of drawing together different ministries with VET responsibilities and other relevant stakeholders.

Social partners' involvement can be described as a continuum between two extremes: social partners run education and training which is provided entirely on-the-job, and schools keep the full responsibility for vocational education and training with no input from social partners. The majority of initial VET programmes fall somewhere in between. Social partners' engagement would typically be strong in apprenticeship systems whereas in school based VET it would be less prominent.

A study by Renold et al. (2016[8]) argues that collaboration between public authorities responsible for education and training and social partners yields optimal outcomes, as all the involved parties benefit. Education authorities are best placed to teach as they have access to teachers, curriculum designers, and students. Employers, on the other hand, possess the latest equipment and technology and the most qualified trainers, and can provide students with real world experience (Renold et al., 2016[8]).

Involvement of social partners in VET policy yields many benefits. The engagement of social partners in VET systems helps to improve labour market outcomes for students and helps to meet the skill needs of employers. Strong VET systems, drawing on social partner engagement, yield benefits to employers by increasing the pool of qualified labour, and benefit students by facilitating their transition to skilled employment (Chapter 3 discusses in more detail benefits associated with work-based learning). In Sweden, a study looking at the provision of work placements in upper secondary VET shows that a strong partnership between the school and local councils improves outcomes from VET (Lundin, 2016[13]). The collective involvement of social partners in VET as a valuable spin-off, can encourage innovation in firms. Social partners are able to reflect upon, and share information, new technologies, production and training methods while updating the components of VET programmes. This effect is stronger for small firms, implying there is a transition of knowledge and innovation from larger companies to smaller ones (Rupietta and Backes-Gellner, 2017[14]).

The role played by social partners and areas of their involvement

A strong VET system involves social partners at all levels where decisions about VET are taken. How the division of responsibility over VET is shared across different bodies depends on individual countries. Social partner engagement occurs at national level, for example in agreeing the main policy features of the VET system: at local and regional level, for example in handling arrangements for work placements. Table 4.1 shows the levels at which social partners are involved across selected OECD countries. Denmark and Finland, like Sweden, maintain arrangements for engaging social partners with individual institutions.

Social partners are often organised by sectors and decide or advise on corresponding VET programmes, for example, social partners representing the construction sector provide input in the design of VET programmes in construction. Sector Education and Training Authorities (SETA) in South Africa provide an example of such sectoral bodies (see Box 4.2).

Table 4.1. The levels at which there exists an institutional framework for social partner engagement (2007 data)

	National	Regional	Institution/Local
Austria	x	x	
Denmark	x		x
Finland	x		x
Germany: apprenticeship	x	x	
Germany: school based VET		x	
Norway	x	x	
Sweden	x		x
Switzerland	x		

Note: The framework for social partners' involvement at the institution level refers to formalised collaboration between institutions and companies at local level. It does not include individual companies providing work placements to students. For example, in Denmark it refers to Local Trade Committees that are set at the institution level.
Source: The OECD International Survey of VET Systems, 2007 – countries' responses (unpublished); Tritscher-Archan, S. (2016[15]), Vocational education and training in Europe – Austria, Cedefop ReferNet VET in Europe reports, http://libserver.cedefop.europa.eu/vetelib/2016/2016_CR_AT.pdf; Andersen, O. and K. Kruse (2016[16]), "Vocational education and training in Europe – Denmark.", *Cedefop ReferNet VET in Europe reports*;, http://www.cedefop.europa.eu/en/publications-and-resources/country-reports/denmark-vet-europe-country-report-2016; Protsch, P. and H. Solga (2016[17]), "The social stratification of the German VET system", *Journal of Education and Work*, Vol. 29/6, pp. 637-661, http://dx.doi.org/10.1080/13639080.2015.1024643.

> ### Box 4.2. Sectoral bodies in South Africa
>
> Following the 1998 Skills Development Act, 23 SETAs were created in 2000, each with their own clearly defined sectors. The members of SETAs represent organised labour and employers, and relevant government departments. After the responsibility for SETAs was transferred from the Department of Labour to the Department for Higher Education and Training, the number of SETAs was reduced to 21 in 2011.
>
> According to the (amended) Skills Development Act, the main functions of SETAs include:
>
> - Analysing skill needs in the sectors through Sector Skills Plans.
> - Implementing the Sector Skills Plan by establishing learning programmes (including VET programmes), approving employers' workplace skills plans and annual training reports, allocating grants to employers, education and training providers (including VET institutions) and workers, monitoring education and training.
> - Promoting learning programmes (including identifying workplaces for practical work experience and supporting the development of learning) and registering agreements for learning programmes.
> - Collecting and disbursing the skills development levy.
> - Liaising with the National Skills Authority, the public employment service, education bodies, provincial skills development forums, and the Quality Council for Trades and Occupations.
>
> Source: OECD (2019[18]), *Community Education and Training in South Africa*, http://dx.doi.org/10.1787/9789264312302-en.

The influence of social partners can be just advisory or consultative, or alternatively can involve full decision-making. In many apprenticeship systems social partners decide on occupational qualifications, corresponding skills, assessment requirements and methods, and the content and delivery of work placements (e.g. in countries such as Austria, Denmark, Germany, Norway and Switzerland). Norway has reinforced the role of social partners in the apprenticeship system by promoting their role from advisory to decision making in relation to the content of training taking place in companies (Utdanningsdirektoratet, 2017[19]). The high level of involvement of the social partners reflects the central role of the employer in apprenticeship: relative to other forms of vocational training, employers therefore have more obligations but also more control.

VET systems engage the social partners in different ways and at different levels (see Table 4.1). Effective arrangements should allow social partners to provide their input into VET regularly, in a timely manner, and in all relevant areas. Box 4.3 describes the form of social partner involvement in Denmark, Norway, South Africa and Sweden. In the four countries, systematic arrangements give the social partners an advisory or decisive role either at national, regional, sectoral or institution level.

Box 4.3. Involvement of social partners in VET

Denmark

National level: Advisory

The national advisory council on vocational upper secondary education and training (*Rådet for de grundlæggende Erhvervsrettede Uddannelser*) meets 8-10 times a year. Among others, it advises the ministry on the establishment of new VET programmes and changes in existing ones, VET programmes to be offered in appretniceship centers, which VET schools should be approved to offer specific VET programmes. The council includes representatives of the social partners, local governments and regional organisations, schools, teachers, and student associations. There are 31 representatives from the employer and employee organisations in the council (Undervisnings Minsteriet, 2018[20]).

National level: Decision making

Around 50 national trade committees (*faglige udvalg*) are responsible for 106 upper secondary VET programmes, and are composed of and funded by employer and employee organisations. Trade committees update existing courses and propose new ones, define learning objectives and final examination standards; decide on the duration of the programme, and the ratio between college-based teaching and practical work in an enterprise; approve enterprises as qualified training establishments and rule on conflicts which may develop between apprentices and the enterprise providing practical training; issue journeyman's certificates in terms of content, assessment and the actual holding of examinations (Andersen and Kruse, 2016[16]).

Institution level: Advisory

Each vocational college (providing school-based education and training) works with at least one local training committee that includes representatives of local employers and employees appointed by national trade committees, and representatives of staff, management and students appointed by colleges. Local training committees work closely with colleges to adapt the content of VET programmes to local needs, strengthen contacts between the college and local employers, and support colleges with the delivery of programmes, for example by securing work placements for students. They also serve as a link between local and national levels, ensuring that national committees have a good overview of local circumstances and that local policy is aligned with national objectives. For example, they assist and advise national trade committees in approving local enterprises as qualified training establishments and in mediating conflicts between apprentices and enterprises (Andersen and Kruse, 2016[16]). The National Committees can hand over obligations to the local trade committees if they are better taken care of at the local level.

Norway

National level: Decision making

At the national level, Norway has a National Council for VET (*Samarbeidsrådet for yrkesopplæring*) and nine Vocational Training Councils (*Faglige råd*), one for each VET programmes, where social partners are represented. These bodies have an advisory role in respect of the first two school-based years of apprenticeships but a decisive role in the last two work-based years of apprenticeships. The government has to take into account the proposals of the social partners unless they are against the law or involve a substantial increase in public spending.

Regional (county) level: Advisory

Social partners sit on 19 Vocational Training Boards (*Yrkesopplæringsnemnda*), one for each county. They provide advice on quality, career guidance, regional development and the provision in the county to meet local labour market needs (Norwegian Centre for International Cooperation in Education (SIU), 2016[21]). County authorities are also responsible for approving enterprises that provide apprenticeship training. While counties are free to develop their own approval procedures, they typically involve social partners from the relevant sector in the process.

South Africa

National level: Advisory

The National Skills Authority (NSA) is a statutory body that was first established in 1999 in terms of Chapter 2 of the Skills Development Act 1998. The NSA brings together representatives from the state, business, labour, community, education and training providers, and employment services. Its role is to advise the minister on skills-related topics, including the VET system, as well as to liaise with the Sector Education and Training Authorities (SETAs, Box 4.2). Its strategic objectives include among others: Provide advice on the National Skills Development Policies to the minister and make inputs in other policy development process related to the Department for Higher Education and Training; Review Skills development legislative framework to support integration of education and training and the national priorities of government; Monitor and evaluate the work of the SETAs and the implementation of the National Skills Development Strategy; Support post-school education and training to realise national priorities. (National Skills Authority, 2021[22]).

Sweden

National: Advisory

The Swedish education system has 18 national upper secondary programmes of which 12 are vocational, all offered either as a school-based programme, or as an apprenticeship. Since 2007, Sweden has developed a permanent national framework for social partners' involvement. In 2010, programme councils for each national upper secondary VET programme were created (Statens offentliga utredningar (SOU), 2015[23]) Thirteen sectoral National Programme Councils (*nationella programråd*) concern themselves with the 12 national vocational programmes. Each council has 8-10 members representing industry, social partners, and sometimes national and regional authorities, and meets around six times a year (Ministry of Education Sweden, 2018[24]). Councils advise the National Agency for Education (the government agency that manages, on behalf of the Ministry of Education, the Swedish school system for youth and adults, including upper secondary VET) on the quality, content and organisation of upper secondary VET for youth and adults, aiming to match VET provision to labour market needs. The councils advise on proposals for new subjects or courses submitted by the National Agency, which may lead to modification of the proposals, or possibly even their abandonment (Equavet, n.d.[25]).

Local: Advisory

Schools are expected to set up collaborative arrangements with one or more Local Programme Councils (*lokala programråd*) in areas corresponding to the VET programmes available in the school. Local Councils are expected to include representatives from local working life, other stakeholders and social partners, and their role is to advise schools on how to adjust VET programmes to local labour market needs and support VET provision, for example, by finding work placements for students. But the influence of local councils varies greatly (Lundin, 2016[13]; Statens offentliga utredningar (SOU), 2015[23]). Local councils are not legally regulated (Ministry of Education Sweden, 2018[24]), and schools are free to organise local councils to fit their needs, so that there is much variation in the quality of local partnerships.

The information provided in Box 4.3 shows that social partners have a say on various aspects of VET. A study by Renold et al., (2016[8]) explores links between social partners' engagements in VET and youth employment outcomes in selected countries. It distinguishes three areas of social partners' involvement:

- curriculum design phase which is about establishing qualifications and examinations standards and setting up quality requirements for VET programmes
- curriculum application which concerns itself with the delivery of the curriculum including provision of training, cost sharing, administration of exams
- and finally there is a curriculum feedback phase during which qualifications are updated.

According to country experts and practitioners involvement of employers in the curriculum design is the most important followed by their engagement in the curriculum application and providing feedback.

The Netherlands and Korea provide contrasting examples of countries with regards to social partners' role in the development of curricula. In the Netherlands, firms and VET schools work together to design a curriculum that fits the needs of the labour market. Skills and knowledge that individual VET programmes should develop in students are described in qualification files. The qualification files have to be updated every four years. Since 2012 their efforts are co-ordinated by the SBB (see Box 3.4 in Chapter 3), a platform facilitating interaction among different stakeholders (Renold et al., 2016[8]). In Korea, involvement of social partners is more limited. Schools are relatively free to create the VET part of the curricula, mostly according to local industry demands. Officially, industrial groups and employers are not involved in curriculum design (Renold et al., 2016[8]), but they might influence the content through negotiations with the VET high schools (Kuczera, Kis and Wurzburg, 2009[26]). There is no formal process for VET high school curriculum updating since it is all done in-school.

In Switzerland, the role of different stakeholders in defining VET qualifications and standards of VET programmes is in fact legally defined (Box 4.4).

Box 4.4. VET ordinances and training plans – VET legal basis in Switzerland

The legal basis for each VET programme in Switzerland can be found in VET ordinances (*Berufsbildungsverordnungen*) issued by the Federal Office for Professional Education and Technology (OPET). These are prepared through the joint efforts of the Confederation, the cantons and the corresponding professional organisations. VET ordinances cover the legally relevant aspects applying to a given occupation: they define the occupational profile, the content of training, the criteria that qualified workers in the occupation must meet, the maximum number of students, and qualification procedures.

All VET ordinances provide for the creation of a Commission for Quality and Development for the given occupation or occupational group. Each Commission is composed of members representing all of the VET partners (Confederation, cantons and professional organisations). Their role is to initiate and adapt training plans for specific VET programmes to the current needs of the labour market. If necessary, the commissions can submit a request to OPET to change the VET ordinance.

Training plans (*Bildungspläne*) form the basis for the vocational teaching concept used for VET programmes. They are used to structure vocational education and training courses and guide vocational teachers and trainers in their work. They define not only the technical but also social and personal skills a student must acquire, the content of education (lessons at vocational schools, range of practical skills taught at the host company and content of industry courses) and specify the respective roles of vocational school, host company and industry training centre in providing these competencies. They also define the process of assessment (Hoeckel, Field and Grubb, 2009[27]).

Source: Hoeckel, K., S. Field and W. Grubb (2009[27]), *OECD Reviews of Vocational Education and Training: A Learning for Jobs Review of Switzerland 2009*, https://dx.doi.org/10.1787/9789264113985-en.

Organisation of employers more broadly

It is easier to engage employers when organised structures, such as employer associations or chambers, exist. Germany has a network of Chambers of Commerce and Industry that represent employers from different sectors. The membership is compulsory as all registered companies in industry, commerce or service are required by law to be a member of one of the Chambers. The Chambers among other things play a key role in provision of VET. They are responsible for providing advisory services to participating companies and supervising company-based training. The Chambers also register apprenticeship contracts, assess the suitability of training firms and monitor their training, assess the aptitude of VET trainers, provide advice to training firms and apprentices, and organise and carry out the final exams.

In some other countries, employers are less organised. This can pose a problem to policy makers as it may not be clear whom they should talk to. The United Kingdom addressed this issue by imposing an obligation on employers who wish to develop an apprenticeship qualification to work together. Employers' input into the definition of qualifications is managed by the Institute for Apprenticeships and Technical Education. The Institute is an employer-led organisation sponsored by the Department for Education, with an independent chair overseeing its work. This chair leads a board of employers, business leaders and their representatives to make sure the apprenticeships and technical products are of the highest quality. The Institute develops, approves, reviews and revises apprenticeships and technical qualifications with employers. A group of employers that wish to set up a new apprenticeship submits an occupation proposal to the Institute. Following the acceptance of the occupational proposal, the standards and assessment as well as funding plan are defined. They are then reviewed by an independent party (Institute for Apprenticeships and Technical Education, 2021[28]).

Conclusions

Some forms of co-ordination between different levels of governance and existing education and training systems is important to foster coherence and collaboration in the VET system, avoid fragmentation, and make the system easy to navigate for students, schools and employers. The issue of co-ordination between various decision-makers may potentially represent a challenge in Brazil as VET schools are run by a range of bodies, including the federal government, states, municipalities, private providers from Sistema S, and other private providers (Itaú Educação e Trabalho, 2021[1]).

Local autonomy is particularly important in large and diverse countries such as Brazil, as it is highly unlikely that one set of rules and standards would suit all localities. Ideally, national/regional prerogatives are combined with local freedom whereby schools can often adapted the content to the local labour markets and student needs. Therefore, the objective should be to ensure co-ordination of various provisions, typically organised at the national or regional level, while allowing for innovation and flexibility at the local level.

Brazil may start with revising existing or creating new VET programmes of excellence through collaboration between selected schools and companies or Sistema S. Stimulating economic development in poorer regions can be one of the goals in setting up such centers of VET excellence. The initiative can be scaled up if successful. Some VET programmes are already run by employers (as part of Sistema S), and many of these programmes are associated with positive labour market outcomes. Involvement of Sistema S in discussions on how the current reform should be rolled out and how to ensure socials partners are involved in provision of VET can help in ensuring the quality of VET.

References

Álvarez-Galván, J. (2015), *A Skills beyond School Review of Costa Rica*, OECD Reviews of Vocational Education and Training, OECD Publishing, Paris, https://dx.doi.org/10.1787/9789264233256-en. [11]

Andersen, O. and K. Kruse (2016), "Vocational education and training in Europe – Denmark.", *Cedefop ReferNet VET in Europe reports;*, http://www.cedefop.europa.eu/en/publications-and-resources/country-reports/denmark-vet-europe-country-report-2016 (accessed on 16 July 2018). [16]

ECBO (2016), *VET in the Netherlands*, Cedefop, http://www.cedefop.europa.eu/files/4142_en.pdf. [9]

Equavet (n.d.), *Equavet : The role of stakeholders in the quality assurance of the design of national qualifications Sweden1*, https://www.eqavet.eu/EU-Quality-Assurance/Case-Studies/The-role-of-stakeholders-in-the-quality-assurance/Sweden-1 (accessed on 17 July 2018). [25]

Fazekas, M. and S. Field (2013), *A Skills beyond School Review of Switzerland*, OECD Reviews of Vocational Education and Training, OECD Publishing, Paris, https://dx.doi.org/10.1787/9789264062665-en. [4]

Hoeckel, K., S. Field and W. Grubb (2009), *OECD Reviews of Vocational Education and Training: A Learning for Jobs Review of Switzerland 2009*, OECD Reviews of Vocational Education and Training, OECD Publishing, Paris, https://dx.doi.org/10.1787/9789264113985-en. [27]

Hoeckel, K. and R. Schwartz (2010), *OECD Reviews of Vocational Education and Training: A Learning for Jobs Review of Germany 2010*, OECD Reviews of Vocational Education and Training, OECD Publishing, Paris, https://dx.doi.org/10.1787/9789264113800-en. [5]

Institute for Apprenticeships and Technical Education (2021), , https://www.instituteforapprenticeships.org/. [28]

Itaú Educação e Trabalho (2021), *Planejamento Estratégico*. [1]

Kis, V. (2017), *A Skills Beyond School Commentary on Viet Nam*, OECD, Paris, https://www.oecd.org/education/skills-beyond-school/countrystudies.htm#Vietnam. [3]

Kuczera, M., T. Bastianić and S. Field (2018), *Apprenticeship and Vocational Education and Training in Israel*, OECD Reviews of Vocational Education and Training, OECD Publishing, Paris, https://dx.doi.org/10.1787/9789264302051-en. [2]

Kuczera, M., V. Kis and G. Wurzburg (2009), *OECD Reviews of Vocational Education and Training: A Learning for Jobs Review of Korea 2009*, OECD Reviews of Vocational Education and Training, OECD Publishing, Paris, https://dx.doi.org/10.1787/9789264113879-en. [26]

Lundin, C. (2016), *Det arbetsplatsförlagda lärandet på gymnasieskolans yrkesprogram*, Skovlerket, https://www.skolverket.se/sitevision/proxy/om-oss/publikationer-och-nyhetsbrev/sok-publikationer/svid12_5dfee44715d35a5cdfa2899/55935574/wtpub/ws/skolbok/wpubext/trycksak/Blob/pdf3643.pdf?k=3643 (accessed on 17 July 2018). [13]

Ministry of Education Sweden (2018), "Review of VET in Sweden. Background report". [24]

National Skills Authority (2021), *National Skills Authority*, http://www.nationalskillsauthority.org.za/. [22]

Norwegian Centre for International Cooperation in Education (SIU) (2016), "Vocational Education and Training in Europe – Norway", *Cedefop ReferNet VET in Europe Reports*, Cedefop, http://libserver.cedefop.europa.eu/vetelib/2016/2016_CR_NO.pdf. [21]

OECD (2021), *Vocational Education and Training in Thailand*, OECD Reviews of Vocational Education and Training, OECD Publishing, Paris, https://dx.doi.org/10.1787/cc20bf6d-en. [10]

OECD (2020), *OECD Economic Surveys: Brazil 2020*, OECD Publishing, Paris, https://dx.doi.org/10.1787/250240ad-en. [12]

OECD (2019), *Community Education and Training in South Africa*, Getting Skills Right, OECD Publishing, Paris, http://dx.doi.org/10.1787/9789264312302-en. [18]

Protsch, P. and H. Solga (2016), "The social stratification of the German VET system", *Journal of Education and Work*, Vol. 29/6, pp. 637-661, http://dx.doi.org/10.1080/13639080.2015.1024643. [17]

Renold, U. et al. (2016), "Feasibility Study for a Curriculum Comparison in Vocational Education and Training: Intermediary Report II: Education-Employment Linkage Index", *KOF studies*, https://doi.org/10.3929/ethz-a-010696087. [8]

Rupietta, C. and U. Backes-Gellner (2017), "High quality workplace training and innovation in highly developed countries", *Economics of Education Working Paper Series*, https://ideas.repec.org/p/iso/educat/0074.html. [14]

SBB (2021), *About SBB*, https://s-bb.nl/en/. [7]

Standing Conference of the Ministers of Education and Cultural Affairs (2018), *The Education System in the Federal Republic of Germany 2017/2018. Description of the responsibilities, structures and developments in education policy for the exchange of information in Europe*, https://www.kmk.org/dokumentation-statistik/informationen-zum-deutschen-bildungssystem/dossier-englisch.html. [6]

Statens offentliga utredningar (SOU) (2015), "Välja yrke", https://www.regeringen.se/rattsliga-dokument/statens-offentliga-utredningar/2015/11/sou-201597/. [23]

Tritscher-Archan, S. (2016), *Vocational education and training in Europe – Austria*, Cedefop ReferNet VET in Europe reports, http://libserver.cedefop.europa.eu/vetelib/2016/2016_CR_AT.pdf. [15]

Undervisnings Minsteriet (2018), *Om Rådet for de grundlæggende Erhvervsrettede Uddannelser - Undervisningsministeriet*, https://uvm.dk/erhvervsuddannelser/ansvar-og-aktoerer/raad-og-udvalg/reu/om-reu (accessed on 29 August 2018). [20]

Utdanningsdirektoratet (2017), *Retningslinjer for samarbeid – SRY, faglige råd og Udir*, https://fagligerad.files.wordpress.com/2016/05/retningslinjer-samarbeid-for-sry-fagligerad-udir.pdf. [19]

5 Assessment and certification in vocational education and training

This chapter looks at international experience with vocational education and training (VET) assessment and certification. It discusses the need for standardisation and independence, as well as the importance of 'holistic' assessments. It looks at the role of employers and trade unions in planning and undertaking assessments, and how this can enhance the quality of assessment, and improve the credibility of certification.

The role of assessment and certification in vocational education and training

The central aim of vocational education and training (VET) programmes is to provide graduates with the competences necessary to do specific jobs, and alongside the competences, the certification which assures employers and other stakeholders that graduates have those competences. Summative assessment, typically a precondition of certification, is therefore a key part of VET programmes, ensuring not only that job competences are part of a qualification and the taught curriculum, but also that the required competences have been acquired by graduates. Effective assessment is therefore a necessary element of a strong VET system.

In Brazil, as in other countries, the confidence of employers and trade unions – the social partners - in VET programmes is therefore likely to depend, among other factors, on the quality of assessment systems. Direct employer involvement in the design and implementation of assessments will in itself do much to enhance that confidence, and this is discussed throughout the chapter.

However, the objectives of assessment go wider than just demonstrating occupational competence to employers. Other objectives of such assessments include:

- As formative assessment, to support and inform the learning process, through feedback to both learner and teacher.
- To motivate students, recognising and rewarding their learning, and to signal the mix of competences they need to acquire.
- To demonstrate the wider and deeper competences that go beyond immediate job skills, and underpin the further learning that will be necessary as jobs change and individual careers develop.
- As aggregated statistics, to provide information about the performance of training providers, and the impact of changing policy and practice.

Assessment and certification in the wider VET context: Occupational standards and qualifications

Assessment and certification must build on an understanding of particular occupations and the competences they require. Countries often maintain a formal arrangement for identifying and classifying occupational standards. These standards describe occupations and the competences they require. Sometimes they may also be linked to associated qualifications/certifications. Passing an assessment, which tests out possession of these competences, then often becomes a precondition of certification. In Brazil, the Ministry of Labour maintains the "*Classificação Brasileira de Occupações*" (CBO) or the Brazilian Classification of Occupations. The CBO lists existing occupations in the Brazilian formal labour market, briefly describes the job content, as well as the education and experience requirements in terms of qualification level and field-of-study (OECD, 2018[1]). An example from another country of occupational standards and how governments may work with employers and unions to manage the system is given in Box 5.1.

> **Box 5.1. Occupational standards, qualifications and the assessment system in Estonia: Systematic involvement of the productive sector**
>
> In Estonia, the education ministry delegates responsibility for the professional qualifications system to a qualifications authority (*Kutsekoda*), steered by representatives of employers, unions and government working together. This body organises and co-ordinates the activities of professional councils and keeps the register of professional qualifications.
>
> Professional councils, representing 14 sectors, approve and update professional standards, and include representatives of trade unions, employer organisations, professional associations and public authorities. The professional standards set out the content of different occupations and the competences, which are expected of individuals in those occupations.
>
> Professional councils select awarding bodies (public and private) to organise the assessment of competences and issue qualifications. The awarding bodies are selected for five years through a public competition organised by the qualifications authority. VET providers may also be given the right to award qualifications, if the curriculum of the institution complies with the professional standard and is nationally recognised.
>
> To manage assessments, the awarding body sets up a committee involving sectoral stakeholders: employers, employees, training providers, and representatives of professional associations. Often it also includes customer representatives and other interested parties. This ensures impartiality in awarding qualifications. The committee approves assessment procedures, including examination materials, decides on awarding qualifications, and resolves complaints. It may set up an assessment committee that evaluates the organisation and results of the assessment and reports to the qualifications committee. The assessment committee verifies to what extent the applicant's competences meet the requirements of the professional qualification standards. A person's competences can be assessed and recognised regardless of whether they have been acquired through formal, non-formal or informal learning.
>
> Source: Adapted from CEDEFOP (2014[2]), *VET in Europe: Country Report 2014*, https://www.cedefop.europa.eu/en/publications-and-resources/country-reports/estonia-vet-europe-country-report-2014. See also Kutsekoda Estonian Qualifications Authority (2021[3]), Estonian Qualifications Authority, https://www.kutsekoda.ee/en/.

Certification: The context for assessment

Certification usually depends on completion of approved training, as well as an assessment. In the context of vocational qualifications, certification is typically intended to confirm that an individual is occupationally competent. It also provides additional information. For example:

- In England (United Kingdom), the T-Level vocational certificate will include separate grades for the core component, using A* to E, and for each occupational specialism, shown as pass, merit or distinction (DfE, 2020[4]).
- Sometimes, more than one certificate is issued to reflect the different components of a programme and the connected assessments. For example in Germany, the graduating apprentice receives three certificates: one reflects an examination of professional competence, one a report of performance in the vocational school, and one a report on the apprentice's performance by their training employer.

Certification commonly follows success in an assessment, but often depends on more than just an assessment, such as completion of a learning programme, or requirements for employment experience or placements with an employer. For example, upper secondary VET programmes in Brazil will be subject to various quality requirements, regarding curricula, number of learning hours, vocational teachers and so forth, that are designed to ensure that the training is of good quality. The assessment, alongside these requirements on the training programme, should provide assurance that those passing through the programme and successful in the assessment are competent. Employer involvement in assessment therefore sits alongside employer involvement in the design and delivery of the training programme in underpinning the credibility of certification.

Sometimes certification may depend almost entirely on assessment. In theory, if an assessment successfully tests everything required for occupational competence, it should not matter what type of formal or informal training has been undertaken. That theory underpins very radical recent reforms in Finland that remove a lot of regulation on training programmes (Box 5.2). But assessments are fallible: even with the strongest assessments, those who are not competent may pass assessments, and those who are competent may fail. So while we should aim for the best possible assessment, that aim needs to be tempered by realism.

> **Box 5.2. In Finland, deregulating the pathways to qualification**
>
> In 2018, Finland made large changes in its system of vocational education. At upper secondary level, a fixed three-year programme was replaced by a more 'personalised' model for both adults and young people. Under this model, students may start the programme at any point during the year, and follow an individual study path of no fixed length, adapted to their individual needs and allowing for recognition of prior learning. Increasing emphasis is placed on virtual learning environments, and work-based learning. These different study paths all lead to the same final qualifications. Assessment, which previously involved some emphasis on examinations, will now give primacy to the demonstration of vocational skills in the workplace (Finnish Ministry of Education and Culture, 2017[5]; Karttunen, 2018[6]).
>
> At first sight, the attractions of this model, in responding to individual student needs, encouraging lifelong learning, and meeting employer needs are substantial. However it is asking a lot of local providers to expect them to manage an infinite variety of learning pathways while maintaining consistent national standards.
>
> Adapted from Field, S. (2021[7]), *A World Without Maps: Assessment in Technical Education*, https://www.gatsby.org.uk/uploads/education/reports/pdf/assessment-in-technical-education-simon-field.pdf

One special type of assessment, linked closely to certification is recognition of prior learning (RPL), which is designed to help adults with work experience or unrecognised training, to obtain partial or full recognition and certification of what they already know how to do. Previous OECD work identified some gaps in Brazilian provision in this field relative to other countries (Box 5.3).

Box 5.3. Recognition of prior learning: How Brazil compares

In Brazil, while there is a decentralised programme for the formal recognition of prior learning, called "Rede CERTIFIC", this programme was never fully developed and implemented. Very few schools became members of the "CERTIFIC" network and the number of certificates issued remains very small. As a consequence, individuals have no means of proving that the experience and knowledge they have accumulated over time is sufficient to enrol for training courses with entry requirements.

In response, the OECD recommended that a large-scale programme for the recognition of prior learning should be developed and implemented. Public awareness campaigns to highlight the benefits of participation in adult training should also be conducted. Such a system can improve the Brazilian adult learning system in two respects: (i) it would contribute to engage older workers into adult learning, who might be excluded from the programme on the basis that they lack entry requirements; and (ii) it would establish a standardised framework to select candidates who do not possess formal qualifications, minimising the amount of discretion by staff working for different adult learning providers (OECD, 2018[1]).

Many countries have a system of RPL in place (Field and Guez, 2018[8]):

- In **France**, a 2002 law establishes an individual right to the recognition of professional experience (*validation des acquis de l'expérience*, VAE) in the acquisition of an academic qualification. This allows an individual to obtain part or all the qualification based on professional experience. The candidate prepares an application documenting their relevant professional experience, which is then examined by a panel including both academic and professional members. The panel may then either grant the full qualification, or alternatively set out the courses that need to be followed by the candidate to complete the qualification. The qualification obtained is the same as can be obtained through academic study.
- **Mauritius** implemented an RPL system in 2009. It follows the qualifications set up in its NQF and has been widely accepted by all stakeholders, so that RPL has been progressively extended to a larger range of sectors. First, the application for RPL is pre-screened. Then, if the pre-screening is successful, an RPL facilitator is assigned and helps the candidate build a portfolio, which collects the candidate's employment history, evidence of skills, and any relevant experience, within a period of three months. The portfolio can include formal education results, samples of work produced, performance appraisal reports and references, photographs of work activities and written testimonials. After submission of the portfolio, an assessment against a selected qualification is carried out through an interview. If the applicant meets the standards, the assessment leads to the delivery of a full or partial qualification In Mauritius, RPL thus serves as a bridge and feeder to further and higher education.
- The University of the Western Cape, in **South Africa**, provides RPL services to thousands of students. There are two ways for candidates to apply for admission to the university through RPL. First, the portfolio development course is a sixteen-week programme in which students attend lectures, write assignments and document their learning history to produce a portfolio that will be assessed in the application process. The course also prepares students for interviews and includes mentoring support. Second, Tests for Access and Placement includes two different tests: the first one assesses applicants' motivation and level of prior learning, while the second (the National Benchmark Test) evaluates their potential to cope with the level of academic skills, writing and numeracy that are needed in higher education.

Building valid and reliable assessments

Any vocational assessment may be conceived as involving: first, a set of *tasks* which candidates are expected to perform, and second, *procedures* for evaluating these candidates on the basis of those tasks. So, for example, academic assessment tasks might often involve examination questions involving written answers, while the procedures for evaluation might involve a marking framework and guidelines, as well as organisational features such as trained examiners, and moderation and appeal procedures. For example in England, the assessment plan for a pipe welder includes tasks such as welding operations and health and safety procedures, while the procedures include rules such as the requirement that for an overall pass, the candidate must pass every assessment module. The outcome depends both on the tasks and the procedures (IfATE, 2021[9]).

Assessments are often appraised in terms of reliability (consistent standards) and validity (assessing the right competences) (New Zealand Ministry of Education, 2021[10]; Darr, 2005[11]).

- Validity refers to the capacity of an assessment to accurately measure what it intends to measure. For a vocational assessment this will mean the capacity to accurately measure the ability of the candidate to perform well in the target occupation.
- Reliability refers to consistency, so that the assessment applies the same standards to different individuals, in different contexts, with different assessors and assessment bodies, and does not change over time. Various quantitative measures of reliability are available.

These two characteristics are different, but not independent. A highly valid assessment is necessarily also reliable, since a very inconsistent measure cannot yield accurate predictions of occupational competence. However a reliable vocational assessment may have low validity (see Box 5.4 for France).

Box 5.4. Reliability, validity and medical training in France

In France, the six-year vocational programme for doctors used to terminate in a single national written examination, the *épreuves classantes nationales* (ECN). Marks received in this examination had a big influence on the career of a doctor, as places in more or less prestigious hospitals and specialities are determined by the marks. While this national examination removes the risk of variation in marking between test centres – a critical point given the influence the examination has on a medical career – it is being reformed because it is deemed to have insufficient emphasis on medical skills as opposed to knowledge. The new assessment tools will include simulations to measure practical medical and interpersonal skills. So an assessment of high reliability but questionable validity (the national examination) is being reformed in order to improve validity, but possibly also reducing reliability.

Source: Adapted from Field, S (2021[7]), *A World Without Maps: Assessment in Technical Education*, https://www.gatsby.org.uk/uploads/education/reports/pdf/assessment-in-technical-education-simon-field.pdf.

Standardisation

In academic education, strenuous efforts are made to standardise assessments by making both assessment tasks and procedures as stable and consistent as possible. This often involves national written examinations, with strictly controlled nationally organised procedures for appraising performance in these examinations so that all candidates face the same or very similar assessment tasks and are marked in the same way. In the context of VET, there are similar grounds for pursuing as much standardisation as possible, but, as will be explained below, there are some countervailing considerations. To begin with, it is worth emphasising what *can* readily be standardised in a vocational assessment.

- The *procedures* for assessment in the sense of criteria for assessment, persons involved in the assessment, rules for resits and retakes and so forth should be, and usually are, designed to be as consistent as possible. Arrangements such as validation and external assessment, and other quality assurance measures, are often designed to reinforce procedural consistency and therefore reliability. In the Spanish Basque country for example, a calibration procedure is used to ensure that teachers use similar assessment and grading criteria. Every two years, groups of vocational teachers are brought together to correct the same written assignment independently and then compare outcomes, discussing their proposed grades and seeking consensus. The results of this grading discussion are recorded for future use (CEDEFOP, 2015[12]).
- Some knowledge-based VET assessment *tasks* can readily be standardised. The knowledge element of occupational competence can often be appraised through written tests. Thus an electrician needs to understand the physics of electricity. This theoretical or knowledge dimension is often classroom taught, and typically assessed through written examinations, which may be standardised. In New Zealand, for example, trainee electricians must undergo a practical assessment and a final computer-based examination. The practical assessment is undertaken in a decentralised way by different training providers, with results submitted to the Electrical Workers Registration Board for approval. The final examination for an electrician involves a multiple choice, computer-based test undertaken in an examination centre. Candidates must have undertaken an approved course with an approved training provider to be eligible to take the examination. Resits are allowed but after three failures within three months, some retraining will be required (Electrical Workers Registration Board, 2021[13]).
- Some practical skills may also be assessed in a standardised way, by defining a set of tasks expected of all candidates, and requiring candidates to undertake those tasks under controlled conditions, such as in a regional vocational assessment centre. In England this takes place through the AM2 test (National Electrotechnical Training, 2021[14]). In Switzerland, assessment of the practical skills of an apprentice involves first, an examination related to a standardised set of tasks or project which are the same for all candidates in the occupational field, and are usually conducted at the same time; and second, an individual practical project completed at the workplace and agreed with the individual employer. The project is presented by the apprentice to the examiners who award the grade (see (International Labour Organisation, 2020[15])).

Also in Brazil, standardisation is common in adult VET- see Box 5.5.

Box 5.5. Standardised assessment in SENAI programmes in Brazil

In SENAI courses, as soon as 80% of the training course has been completed, students can be asked to sit an on-line test to evaluate whether they have acquired the necessary skills for the occupation they are training for. Such tests are prepared by the faculty of SENAI and consist of multiple-choice questions. They assess specific skills that students should have developed during the training, but also, general and management competencies. On-line tests are common across all SENAI schools in the country and standardized. Students are also required to fill a short background questionnaire so as to provide information on their socio-economic context. However, such online tests have limitations in assessing real work challenges. Since 2017, a subset of the students who take the on-line test are also selected for a practical test. The practical test consists of presenting students with a concrete problem that could come up in their work routine and assessing the proposed solution. (OECD, 2018[1])

Source: OECD (2018[1]), *Getting Skills Right: Brazil* , https://dx.doi.org/10.1787/9789264309838-en.

In fields where working practice involves human subjects (as in healthcare), or expensive machinery (such as aircraft or CNC machines), technology-assisted simulation, where no persons or expensive machines are at risk, has large attractions, including for the standardisation of assessment. Simulation also allows both practice and assessment in the handling of rare but critical events, such as medical emergencies, or engine failures for pilots. A controlled set of challenges can be offered, both to train students, and subsequently to assess their skills. A substantial literature has emerged on the use of such technology, recognising both its potential and its limitations (for example in simulating the capacity to address interpersonal challenges). Simulation technology may also facilitate standardisation in assessment, so that candidates face the same, or similar challenges in a final examination (Ahn and Nyström, 2020[16]). In the reform of medical education in France, designed to enhance the assessment of practical skills, the intention is to use simulation technology, notably programmable robotic patients, not only to train but also to assess medical students (see (Ministère de Solidarité et de Santé, 2018[17])) and Box 5.6.

Work-embedded assessment tasks: A challenge to standardisation?

In the productive sector, ability to do the job is assessed most directly by looking at how well candidates perform authentic work tasks. For example, not just undertaking a standard task like fixing a leaking pipe in the case of a plumber, but also negotiating with a client, diagnosing the plumbing fault, working and communicating with other artisans, costing and scheduling the repair task, and dealing with unexpected vocational, practical and human challenges in the course of the work. Some soft competences and dispositions like teamwork, resilience and conscientiousness are critical to success in many workplaces (an issue further discussed below). In response, to address occupational competence more fully, assessment tasks embedded in the everyday reality of the workplace are utilised in many VET systems (as in Brazil recently in the SENAI assessments described above). In the Netherlands, this approach has been more fully embraced, as set out in Box 5.6.

The difficulty is that such authentic work tasks are, as many commentators have recognised, extremely difficult to standardise (Stanley, 2017[18]; Yu and Frempong, 2012[19]). As a result, there is always some tension between the objective of a fully standardised assessment delivering full reliability, and an assessment employing tasks which are fully realistic and reflective of authentic working practice.

> #### Box 5.6. Work-embedded assessment projects in the Netherlands
>
> In the Netherlands, the practical component of vocational assessment at upper secondary level is linked to work placements. A project, associated with a real professional activity, is chosen and approved (by the student, trainer at school and workplace trainer) at the beginning of the school year. The candidate must then carry out the project within the company (whilst treated as a regular employee) over a period of around six weeks. The student prepares a written report and a presentation, in which they are expected to demonstrate mastery of the required learning outcomes. Assessment and grading are undertaken by a minimum of two people to ensure impartiality – typically the school and workplace trainers. In their final year, students take part in three of four of these projects. This practical assessment is a component of a decentralised assessment system where the training providers themselves (or regional authorities) develop examination questions and tasks. However, since 2014 the certification exams in English, Dutch, and Mathematics which form part of the vocational programmes have been centralised.
>
> Source: CEDEFOP (2015[12]), "Ensuring the Quality of Certification in Vocational Education and Training", *Cedefop Research Paper*, No. 51, https://data.europa.eu/doi/10.2801/79334.

Competing advantages of standardised and work-embedded assessment tasks

Drawing on all the points made above, Table 5.1 summarises the pros and cons of using standardised tasks in VET assessments as opposed to assessment linked to more authentic working practice. Standardised tasks offer more confidence that the assessment applies the same standards to all candidates, and are often suitable for the cognitive, knowledge part of occupational competence, as they can be assessed using written examinations. Comparative performance of training providers on standardised tasks also provides helpful data aiding the quality assurance of providers. Conversely work-embedded assessment tasks are much more closely aligned with the realities of working practice, and better suited to the appraisal of certain higher level occupational competences and dispositions. Finally, and critically, employers obviously have a more natural role in both devising and undertaking such work-embedded assessments.

Table 5.1. The relative advantages of standardised and work-embedded tasks in assessment in vocational education and training

	Standardised tasks	Work-embedded tasks
Confidence that the same standards are applied to all candidates	Yes	More challenging
Suitability to cognitive aspects of competence	Yes	More challenging
Provide good data on the performance of training providers	Yes	More challenging
Realistic work tasks assessed	More challenging	Yes
Suitability to the assessment of soft cross curricular competences like teamwork	More challenging	Yes
Engagement of employers in assessment	More challenging	Yes

There is a strong case for work-embedded assessment as the most credible test available for occupational competence. But it would be self-defeating if the effect were to permit so much variation that pure luck comes to determine the difficulty of the assessment task, and hence who passes the assessment. In response to these competing considerations, a balance may be struck through steps such as the following:

- As discussed above, the knowledge-based part of occupational competence can be assessed in a standardised way through written tests.
- Also as discussed above, the procedures used to assess the work-embedded tasks may be subject to standardisation.
- Assessment tasks, even if variable and work-embedded, may still be required to meet standardised requirements, for example to ensure that they always allow for the assessment of the key elements of occupational competence.
- Standardised and work-embedded assessment tasks may be blended in a composite assessment. Sometimes the knowledge part of occupational competence can naturally be tested through a standardised national examination. In the Czech Republic, for example students in vocational upper secondary programmes are assessed through a combination of national exams and practical tests devised and managed by local vocational schools (CEDEFOP, 2015[12]).

Federal and decentralised assessment standards

In many countries with decentralised and federal governance arrangements, like Brazil, standardisation of assessment may take place at sub-national level. Clearly if qualifications/certifications are defined sub-nationally, then the assessments need to follow suit. However if assessments procedures and tasks are agreed more locally than the associated qualification, an issue arises of whether the qualification obtained through one locally determined assessment requires the same standards as the same qualification obtained in a different area and therefore subject to a different assessment. Some of these challenges are apparent in some Italian qualifications (Box 5.7).

Conversely, in some federal systems, national assessments can be designed so as to address some regional differences in qualifications and programmes, and deliver a nationally recognised certification as in Canada. Although apprenticeship is managed and delivered by the different provinces and territories, a national assessment (the Red Seal examination) is developed in collaboration to meet requirements of all 13 provinces and territories. In this way, apprentices qualifying in one province or territory may obtain a nationally recognised endorsement to their certification in their chosen trade (see also Box 5.7 and Chapter 4).

> **Box 5.7. In Italy and Canada, assessments reflect and address regional variations**
>
> **In Italy**, alongside regular school-based upper secondary vocational education, there are regionally organised vocational programmes (IFP). The assessments for these programmes vary from region to region, but some elements are common. There are three types of tests, theory, practical, and oral, developed by institutions in some regions, and at regional level in others. Sometimes theory tests are prepared regionally and practical tests at institution level. The final mark is a weighted sum of marks from the last year of study, the final examination and sometimes an employer appraisal from a placement. The weighting varies between regions (Eurydice, 2020[20]).
>
> **In Canada,** apprenticeship is managed by the separate provinces and territories, but a national examination is used to assess candidates in each of the Red Seal trades. Successful candidates receive a Red Seal endorsement to their certification which is recognized across Canada. The Red Seal examination, which is based on national occupational standards, contains between 100 and 150 multiple-choice questions, to be answered during a 4-hour examination. Around three-quarters of candidates pass the exam (Canadian Council of Directors of Apprenticeship, 2016[21]).

Assessing the right set of skills at the right time

Holistic vs atomistic assessment

A second distinction, related to that between standardised and work-embedded assessment tasks, is that between holistic and atomistic assessment. In working life, employers most naturally assess potential recruits, 'in the round', or holistically, to decide whether they are capable of doing the job. Conversely, atomistic approaches break down occupational competence and assessments into their elements and check them off one by one. The linkage with the standardised/work-embedded distinction flows from how holistic assessment usually requires an authentic work-embedded assessment task. However atomistic approaches to assessment can be standardised or, alternatively, work-embedded.

The departure point for atomistic assessment is an atomistic approach to occupational competence and standards. This involves breaking down an occupation into the set of competences required to undertake that occupation. The competences include, for example in the case of a blacksmith, different elements of knowledge, such as knowledge of materials used, different skills such as design drawing, and dispositions and behaviours, such as a commitment to safety in the workplace. Full occupational competence is then defined in terms of the possession of this list of competences (Annex 5.A).

Given such a list of competences, an assessment may be designed to measure acquisition of each competence on this list. This establishes a transparent link between assessment and the list of competences which constitute occupational competence, a big advantage for quality assurance. It also allows assessments, for example, to identify a set of core competences which are always necessary, while having a more optional approach to other competences. Elements of knowledge can also be separately assessed from other competences – for example in a written examination that is separate from the assessment of practical skills. For a blacksmith in England, the associated assessment plan is described in Annex 5.A.

Under a *holistic* approach, occupational competence is sometimes associated with a professional identity that is over and above the tasks required in the job and the associated competences – competences which may come and go with changing technology and workplace organisation. This approach may depend partly on the profession: professions like teaching and nursing are associated with strong professional missions and values, independent of the changing set of competences necessary to deliver those missions. In other professions, like IT technicians, professional missions are harder to define. Given a professional identity, the argument is that occupational competence needs to be assessed in relation to that identity, rather than in relation to more contingent competences.

A separate argument for holistic assessment is that real work requires not just a list of separate competences, but also the capacity to apply a judiciously chosen set of those competences in response to complex and sometimes unexpected practical challenges. Such a high-level capacity is both critical to success in the workplace and more naturally addressed by holistic assessment. The terminology can be confusing, as such capacities are variably characterised, in overlapping but varying notions, as 'soft', '21st century', 'meta-cognitive' and 'cross-curricular' skills and competences. Thus, for example:

- In Scotland (United Kingdom), 'meta-skills', including self-management, social intelligence and innovation, have been argued to be the key to future-proofing the skills system in Scotland. It is maintained that such competences are not easily taught in a classroom, and they can most naturally be developed in a work-based context. By the same token, they are difficult to measure, and therefore assess, except in the context of regular work, or special projects that closely mimic the demands of ordinary work (Skills Development Scotland and Centre for Workbased Learning, 2018[22]).
- Bjaelde, Lauridsen and Lindberg (2018[23]) describe how assessments of higher-level professional competences (often at tertiary level) require candidates to solve 'authentic' work problems with competences that may include, for example, teamwork, critical thinking and interpersonal skills.

Table 5.2 summarises the pros and cons of atomistic and holistic approaches. More atomistic approaches make it easier to check that all required skills for an occupation have been tested, and allow periodic modular assessments associated with each training module to check on the acquisition of the competence(s) developed in each module. Standardisation is also facilitated, for example through agreement on the relative importance of different competences in assessment. Conversely, holistic approaches more naturally fit with the assessment of real work tasks; they can also more readily capture the soft skills necessary to solve multi-faceted problems. Employers will also recognise such assessment tasks more naturally since they are work based.

Table 5.2. The relative advantages of atomistic and holistic approaches to assessment in vocational programmes

	Atomistic assessment	Holistic assessment
Confidence that all relevant competences have been identified and assessed	Yes	More challenging
Allow for modular assessment and partial credit	Yes	More challenging
Support standardised assessment	Yes	More challenging
Realistic work tasks assessed – consistent with a holistic view of professional identity	More challenging	Yes
Suitability to the assessment of soft skills, in which candidates deploy a mix of competences to solve a problem	More challenging	Yes
Engagement of employers in assessment	More challenging	Yes

The atomistic and holistic approaches are not mutually exclusive. Occupational competence involves both atomistic elements of knowledge and skills, and the capacity make use of these competences to solve workplace challenges. With this point in mind, it is natural and desirable for assessments to reflect both approaches. One example of this type of blend is the model of Luxembourg (Box 5.8).

> **Box 5.8. A blend of periodic modular and holistic final assessment in Luxembourg**
>
> In Luxembourg, the vocational education system has many similarities with that of Germany, with a dual system of apprenticeship at upper secondary level, alongside some school-based vocational programmes. Summative assessment involves both periodic and a final assessment (European Alliance for Apprenticeships, 2021[24]):
>
> - *Modular periodic assessment.* The programmes are organised in modules, each leading to a subset of competences for a specific occupation. Each module is assessed individually by the vocational education teacher or the in-company trainer responsible for the associated teaching or training. The apprentice must pass a fixed proportion of mandatory modules before entering the final assessment.
> - *Final holistic assessment.* A 2008 reform replaced theoretical and practical final exams with an assessment based on an integrated project, which corresponds to a simulated or real working situation, undertaken over a period of up to 24 hours. The integrated projects are developed and assessed by teams of experts from employer organisations, and vocational teachers from secondary schools (plus some additional assessors). Success in this final assessment leads to certification.

Assessing wider and higher level aspects of occupational competence

As already argued, many countries have been keen to include in their understanding of occupational competence, and reflect in vocational assessments, a range of wider and sometimes higher level competences that go beyond the performance of routine job tasks. These include the soft skills mentioned above, which are needed to fully exploit other competences. They also include basic skills that underpin the capacity to learn: literacy, numeracy and an increasingly important set of digital skills. Such skills underpin further learning, both directly on the job in response to new technological and other developments in the workplace, and to support further formal education and training that may be a necessary element of career development.

In recent decades, partly because of rising educational aspirations, and partly because of increasing skills requirements in the labour market, many vocational programmes and qualifications have been modified to facilitate access to further learning, including higher education (Field and Guez, 2018[8]). Consequently, vocational assessments have needed to give attention not just to the immediate ability to perform on the job, but also to the foundational competences that enable individuals to go on learning. These include numeracy and literacy, but also wider elements of general education. In many countries, this is realised through an upper secondary vocational track, which offers occupation-specific vocational training alongside a substantial component of general education (as also discussed in Chapter 2).

Vocational education and training programmes, as well as including general education, may also directly or indirectly develop other generic competences, including what are commonly called employability skills. These include traits such as self-discipline, honesty and determination and interpersonal skills including teamwork. These skills have significant labour market returns and are often best developed through work-based learning rather than in classrooms (Lerman, 2013[25]). Some of these skills, notably interpersonal skills, have been shown to be of increasing relative importance in England, most plausibly because they correspond to the elements of occupations that are least subject to automation (Adecco,

2017[26]). In the United States, much attention has been given to these competences, and different tools developed to assess them independently of occupation-specific competences (Box 5.9).

> **Box 5.9. The United States is distinctive in making use of free-standing assessments of employability skills**
>
> High schools in the United States do not have the kind of systematic vocational tracks found in many European countries, but in a decentralised system which varies extensively from state to state and school to school, vocational courses are sometimes offered within a broadly comprehensive approach to upper secondary education. Much emphasis is placed on demonstrating that those graduating from high school are 'career and college-ready'.
>
> The 'career-readiness' element of this is subject to diverse assessment tools. In a survey across states, assessments of career readiness were classified into tests of academic, employability and vocational skills. Vocational skills were often assessed through industry recognised certifications of different types. But the United States is distinctive in making extensive use of tests of employability independently of specific vocational domains; these include 'Work Keys' (used in 32 states), and ASVAB (developed by the Department of Defense) also used in 32 states. Very often students themselves, alongside school districts, have to share the costs of these assessments (Centre on Educational Policy, 2013[27]).

Final, periodic and formative assessment

The most common assessment arrangement is a final examination of some type. For example one survey found that nine of eleven European countries surveyed tended to use final assessments in their initial vocational education systems, with the exceptions being Spain and Finland (CEDEFOP, 2015[12]). Such final assessments may be contrasted with 'periodic' assessments undertaken at intervals throughout a learning programme and contributing to the final grade. The arguments for final assessments are simple: they are administratively neat, and better placed than periodic assessment to assess occupational competence as an integrated whole through a holistic assessment, as discussed above. However several factors suggest that there is also value in periodic assessments conducted in the course of a learning programme:

- Formative assessment uses information about learning progress to guide both teachers and learners and thereby support learning. It is therefore necessarily periodic. Much evidence shows that it is a powerful pedagogical tool in general education (Black and Wiliam, 1998[28]), suggesting, although direct evidence is limited, that the same might be true in vocational education (University of Exeter, 2021[29]). In a vocational programme this would, for example, involve the use of periodic tests, with the results fed back to both teacher and student to identify what has been learnt, and what remains to be acquired, thus guiding both teacher and learner in subsequent education and training. Much of this activity may be informal, and take place between the teacher and the student, corresponding to a form of personalised pedagogy. However it can also be formalised: Norway, for example, requires half yearly formative assessments in the consecutive school and workplace segments of apprenticeship programmes. In the final two-year workplace segment, half-year assessments are undertaken by the training supervisor of the apprentice in the training company. The supervisor is expected to explain to the apprentice what competences they still need to acquire, and how they can be acquired (Norwegian Ministry of Education and Research, 2006[30]).
- Periodic assessment can also fit well with a modular approach in which individual elements of occupational competence are separately assessed, facilitating a record of partial learning. This can be used, as in Denmark, as a means of granting the possibility of later completion to those who

- might otherwise drop out with nothing to show for their efforts (Danish Ministry of Education, 2008[31]).
- Earlier chapters of this report have described the critical value of workbased learning as part of vocational programmes. Assessing the learning outcomes from such placements therefore offers a strong indicator of occupational competence, and signals to the student the importance of what can be learnt in the workplace. But as these placements are removed from the main training provider for a vocational programme, assessing the learning outcomes can be challenging. Some countries make assessments of placements a more formal part of overall assessment. For example in France, the 22-week placements that are part of the *baccalauréat professionnel* are subject to an assessment by the teachers from their vocational schools, and represents a varying (according to profession) but substantial contribution to their overall mark in the baccalauréat (Field, 2021[7]).

The case for an element of periodic assessment is stronger in longer programmes, where students need formative feedback in the course of the programme, the risk of dropout is higher, and programmes may involve separate work placements requiring assessment. Thus, for example:

- In German apprenticeships, an assessment normally takes place halfway through the 3-4-year programme to measure the apprentice's acquisition of both theory and practical skills. This is used formatively to provide feedback on learning progress, but, increasingly, it is also used summatively, representing 30-40% of the final mark for the apprenticeship, depending on the profession (see the case of plumber assessment in Germany as set out in Annex 5.B).
- In Swiss apprenticeships, some elements of periodic assessment, reflecting marks given by teachers in inter-company training courses, and in classroom-taught courses, contribute to the final mark in the overall assessment (Field, 2021[7]).
- In Luxembourg, vocational assessment involves a unique mix of modular periodic assessment and a holistic, work-embedded final assessment (Box 5.8).

This points to the need for regular assessment to be followed as part of the VET programmes in Brazil.

Involving all relevant actors in the assessment process

Independence in assessment

The experience of individual teachers and trainers is valuable. In all types of learning, the teachers and trainers responsible for delivering vocational education and training will have most direct knowledge of the performance of trainees, and therefore naturally often play a big role in assessment. In Spain for example, teachers responsible for the different modules of technical programmes participate in assessment board discussions of grading individual students, and deciding whether students can continue to the second year of the programme (CEDEFOP, 2015[12]).

There are two difficulties with relying on local teaching and training staff to conduct assessments. First, these staff have biases — perhaps positive because the performance of the trainee can reflect on their own performance as trainers, or perhaps negative because of conflicts with the trainee. In the context of academic assessments there is evidence of different types of bias (Lee and Newton, 2021[32]). Second, these staff are not always able to apply the same standards as those applied in other contexts. For these two reasons, assessments undertaken by local teaching staff may not be reliable. This means that while it can be valuable to take trainer views into account in assessments, assessments also need a degree of independence from the training process. Such independence can help to enhance reliability, such as when the same external assessor helps to ensure consistent grading of students in different local contexts.

Sometimes independence is realised through nationally or regionally organised examinations, including practical assessments, which are independent of local teachers and trainers. But, as argued earlier, it is often desirable to assess occupational competence in real-world contexts, where local actors are necessarily involved. Some degree of assessment independence can then be realised by mixing an external independent assessment, with an internal element. Some examples follow:

- The Australian state of Victoria is currently running an independent assessment trail in apprenticeship, whereby an independent assessing authority designs, develops and conducts the assessment of the selected eight occupations. Training providers are key partners in piloting the independent assessments (Victoria State Government, 2022[33]).
- In Austria, the final assessment for apprentices includes both a practical and a theoretical component. The practical part of the examination is organised by the regional apprenticeship offices and managed by a board of examiners including a chairperson appointed by the regional advisory board on apprenticeship, one representative of employers and one of employees. The chairperson must be an authorised apprenticeship trainer and at least one other member of the board must be a professional expert (European Alliance for Apprenticeships, 2018[34]).
- In Hungary, responsibility for assessment is shared between the technical school which organises the assessment and an independent examination committee (CEDEFOP, 2015[12]).
- In Korea, technical qualifications are typically awarded after an internal assessment undertaken by a training institute, and an external assessment undertaken by the awarding body (Human Resource Development Korea), with the award depending on an adequate score in both assessments (Coles and Bateman, 2017[35]).

The role of social partners in assessment

The productive sector may be involved both in developing and undertaking assessments. For two good reasons, employers and worker representatives have a major role to play in assessment. First, those with most direct and up-to-date knowledge and experience of workplaces and working requirements are often best able to see what competences are required of workers, and how to test those competences. Second, the involvement of the productive sector in assessment grants it greater credibility, so that associated certifications will be granted more weight by other employers. Given this strong rationale, how can employers get involved in assessment? There are two main ways:

- Through employer involvement in the development of assessments and assessment material (as well as in the underlying qualifications and occupational standards as discussed above), and in managing the whole process of assessment. This type of involvement is almost universal, although the depth of employer involvement is highly variable. One example of how this may work is apprenticeship in England (Box 5.10), where employers are fully involved in the establishment of occupational standards, and in providing a framework for assessment in an 'assessment plan', but employers are not involved in individual assessments.
- Through direct employer involvement, as assessors, in individual assessments. This is much more variable, and in some contexts does not take place at all, with vocational teachers and examiners filling the role. However in some country contexts, the productive sector, through employer and worker representatives, are directly involved in undertaking individual assessments. One notable example is in apprenticeship in Germany, where representatives of both employer organisations and trade unions are *required* to take part in each individual assessment (Annex 5.B).

Employer involvement can make assessments more demanding, and therefore the certification more credible. The involvement of employers in individual assessments is linked to the issue of independence. A sharp distinction must be drawn between the involvement of an individual employer in respect of their own trainees or apprentices, where that employer may have local biases, and the involvement of employer representatives. Employer representatives are independent in the sense that they have nothing personally to gain or lose from an individual passing an assessment. Stakeholders such as employer representatives will however have a 'point of view', in the sense of a legitimate view about the threshold of performance required for a pass in the assessment. As representatives of employers collectively, they may want to set the threshold sufficiently high to be sure that those passing the assessment, and recruited by employers on that basis, are indeed competent. That may mean that they are less forgiving of marginal results in an assessment than other stakeholders, part of the price that is paid for ensuring that the assessment is fully credible. It is notable that the pass rate in the final assessment for apprentices in Germany (where employers are fully involved) is lower than in England (where employers are not routinely involved in undertaking assessments) (Field, 2021[7]).

> Box 5.10. Employer involvement in apprenticeship programmes, certification and assessment in England
>
> In apprenticeship in England, employers take the lead in establishing each apprenticeship qualification, through 'Trailblazer' group led by employers, which identify the competences required for a job (Annex 5.A). The same group also establish an 'assessment plan' setting out in some detail how apprentices are to be assessed at the end of each programme.
>
> The individual employer of an apprentice is involved in assessment in that their approval is a necessary condition for the apprentice to proceed to the assessment. However the assessment itself is delivered by an independent assessment body, chosen from an approved list and selected by the employer of an apprentice.
>
> The assessment plan, which runs to 24 pages in the case of a blacksmith for example, provides detailed guidance on how the assessment is to be conducted, marked and graded, including rules for resits and retakes. While assessment plans vary a lot between occupations, in the case of a blacksmith the plan sets out that assessment should take place through three exercises with equal weight:
>
> - A special project involve the production of a project piece submitted alongside a design/development document.
> - Through a skills demonstration, observed by an independent assessor, involving the completion of all five fundamental blacksmith tasks: a) Forging, b) Thermal welding and cutting c) Machining, d) Bench work, e) Tool making/maintenance.
> - Through a professional discussion underpinned by a workplace journal. This discussion will occupy a minimum of 40 minutes and will involve posing at least 8 competence questions.
>
> Each of these elements is marked fail/pass/distinction using detailed criteria set out in guidance.

Using assessment data to support VET policy implementation and quality assurance

Assessment, as well as supporting individual certifications, has an important role to play in the implementation of the wider VET reforms currently under way in Brazil. Whether these concern vocational teachers, institutions, or employer engagement and work-based learning, their central objective will normally be to deliver well-trained individuals on completion of vocational programmes. Individual assessments, taken collectively, are therefore a vital test of whether such reforms are working – by looking for example at pass rates, or marks and how they are changing. At the institutional level, assessment data can become an indicator of the quality of training provided by that institution. Assessment is therefore a very important part of the evaluation feedback which should attend implementation of VET reform, and changes of teaching practice and policy. Internationally, while academic test data are widely used to evaluate schools and education policies, this practice is less common in the field of VET, partly because of the diversity of vocational fields of study, and partly because assessment (as discussed above) is not always standardised. In Poland, national standardised examinations, with external examiners in regional centres, are used to quality assure the training provided in different regions and schools (Chłoń-Domińczak, 2019[36]).

Assessment data may also be used to support quality assurance. Assessment bodies themselves, as part of internal quality assurance and improvement, can check that their assessments are providing reliable tests of occupational competence, by seeking feedback from employers on any gaps in the competences of newly qualified persons, and addressing such gaps through modifications in assessment and though advice to training providers. For example:

- The government of Western Australia provides guidance on a continuous improvement approach to assessment practice. This requires training providers to regularly review their assessment processes and outcomes to identify flaws and to pinpoint the scope for improvement. This involves a data collection strategy (for example client satisfaction surveys, and data from consultation with learners and industry bodies) to monitor assessments and support quality improvements. When assessment practice is modified to make improvements, the impact of the changes in assessment practice is monitored (Government of Western Australia, 2018[37]).
- in England, the Institute for Apprentices and Technical Education (IfATE) emphasises the importance of continuous improvement in their quality assurance framework, and identify the strongest end-point assessment (EPA) organisations as ones that see themselves as "learning organisations" constantly improving their performance through both internal quality assurance and feedback from stakeholders (IfATE, 2020[38]).

Conclusions

Assessments in the Brazilian VET system should balance different assessment methods. To support reliability, assessments should include some standardised elements, such as written or practical assessment tasks which are the same or very similar for all candidates. However, there is also a need to assess the performance of candidates undertaking realistic work tasks, or pursuing practical projects in the workplace. These tasks or projects should be carefully chosen so as to assess a wide range of competences required for the occupation, including soft and meta- skills such as creativity and teamwork, as well as more narrowly defined occupational skills. In longer programmes, partial assessments undertaken periodically in the course of a programme can play a very constructive role in providing feedback to students and teachers on learning progress, offering partial credit, as well as potentially feeding into a final assessment.

Full involvement of the productive sector, including employers and trade unions, enhances the quality of assessment and certification, and improves the credibility of certification. The productive sector should be involved fully both in the establishment of new curricula in the expanded VET system in Brazil and in updating existing curricula, as well as in the planning of assessment systems, as the productive sector has the most direct and up to date knowledge and experience of required competences. The sector might also be usefully involved in undertaking assessments of individual students, as this will add credibility to the consequent certification of occupational competence.

Brazil should include an independent element in assessment. Those most closely involved in a training programme, including vocational teachers and employers offering work placements, have direct knowledge of students and their capacities and have a useful input into assessment. This should be balanced by independent actors in assessment, who may be less likely to have biases because of any direct interest in the outcome, and who are in a stronger position to ensure consistent standards.

References

Adecco (2017), *AUTONATION. analysing the poential risks and opportunities automation could bring to Britain's labour market*. [26]

Ahn, S. and S. Nyström (2020), "Simulation-based training in VET through the lens of a sociomaterial perspective", *Nordic Journal of Vocational Education and Training*, Vol. 10/1, pp. 1-17, https://www.diva-portal.org/smash/get/diva2:1463505/FULLTEXT01.pdf. [16]

Appreniceship toolbox (2019), *Examination & Certification in Germany*, https://www.apprenticeship-toolbox.eu/standards-matching/examination-certification/90-examination-certification-in-germany (accessed on 25 January 2022). [44]

Australian Skills Quality Authority (2021), *Clauses 1.8 to 1.12—Conduct effective assessment*, https://www.asqa.gov.au/standards/training-assessment/clauses-1.8-to-1.12#:~:text=The%20RTO%20informs%20the%20learner,and%20be%20reassessed%20if%20necessary.&text=Assessment%20is%20flexible%20to%20the,reflecting%20the%20learner's%20needs. [48]

BIBB (2017), , http://www.nuv.cz/uploads/EQAVET/soubory/BIBB_Quality_Assurance_2017.pdf (accessed on 25 January 2022). [43]

BIBB (2017), *Young people study in the company and at school*, https://www.bibb.de/en/77203.php (accessed on 25 January 2022). [46]

BIBB (2016), *Informationen zu Aus- und Fortbildungsberufen*, https://www.bibb.de/dienst/berufesuche/de/index_berufesuche.php/profile/apprenticeship/110512 (accessed on 25 January 2022). [47]

Bjaelde, O., K. Lauridsen and A. Lindberg (2018), *Current Trends in Assessment in Europe: the Way Forward*, https://www.coimbra-group.eu/wp-content/uploads/WP-Trends-in-assessment-FINAL.pdf. [23]

Black, P. and D. Wiliam (1998), "Assessment and Classroom Learning", *Assessment in Education: Principles, Policy and Practice*, Vol. 5/1, pp. 7-7, https://www.gla.ac.uk/t4/learningandteaching/files/PGCTHE/BlackandWiliam1998.pdf. [28]

Bliem, W., A. Petanovitsch and K. Schmid (2016), *Dual Vocational Education and Training in Austria, Germany, Liechtenstein and Switzerland. Comparative Expert Study*, https://ibw.at/bibliothek/id/413/. [45]

Canadian Council of Directors of Apprenticeship (2016), *2016 Annual Review*, http://www.red-seal.ca/docms/2016ar_eng.pdf. [21]

CEDEFOP (2017), *Spotlight on VET: Germany*, https://www.cedefop.europa.eu/en/publications/8116. [40]

CEDEFOP (2015), "Ensuring the Quality of Certification in Vocational Education and Training", *Cedefop Research Paper*, No. 51, Publications Office of the European Union, Luxembourg, https://data.europa.eu/doi/10.2801/79334. [12]

CEDEFOP (2014), *VET in Europe: country report 2014*, https://www.cedefop.europa.eu/en/publications-and-resources/country-reports/estonia-vet-europe-country-report-2014. [2]

Cedefop (2017), *Spotlight on VET in Germany*, Cedefop, https://www.cedefop.europa.eu/files/8116_en.pdf. [41]

Centre on Educational Policy (2013), *Career Readiness Assessments across States: A Summary of Survey Findings*, https://files.eric.ed.gov/fulltext/ED554578.pdf. [27]

Chłoń-Domińczak, A. (2019), *Vocational Education and Training in Europe: Poland*, https://cumulus.cedefop.europa.eu/files/vetelib/2019/Vocational_Education_Training_Europe_Poland_2018_Cedefop_ReferNet.pdf. [36]

Coles, M. and A. Bateman (2017), *Towards Quality Assurance of Technical Vocational Education and Training*, https://unesdoc.unesco.org/in/documentViewer.xhtml?v=2.1.196&id=p::usmarcdef_0000259282&file=/in/rest/annotationSVC/DownloadWatermarkedAttachment/attach_import_3ba90c4c-1cb8-407d-a917-81cb8106ce4b%3F_%3D259282eng.pdf&locale=en&multi=true&ark=/ark:/48223/p. [35]

Danish Ministry of Education (2008), *The Danish Vocational Educational System*, https://www.apprenticeship-toolbox.eu/files/144/Competent-Bodies/133/The_Danish_VET_System.pdf. [31]

Darr, C. (2005), "A hitchhiker's guide to reliability", https://assessment.tki.org.nz/Using-evidence-for-learning/Working-with-data/Concepts/Reliability-and-validity#:~:text=The%20reliability%20of%20an%20assessment,it%20was%20designed%20to%20measure. [11]

DfE (2020), *Guidance. Introduction of T levels. Updated 4 September 2020*, https://www.gov.uk/government/publications/introduction-of-t-levels/introduction-of-t-levels#grading-and-certification. [4]

Electrical Workers Registration Board (2021), *Tuition Courses and Practical Assessments*, https://www.ewrb.govt.nz/becoming-an-electrical-worker/tuition-courses-and-practical-assessments/. [13]

Euler, D. (2013), *Germany's dual vocational trainings: a model for other countries?*, Bertelsmann Stiftung, https://www.bertelsmann-stiftung.de/fileadmin/files/BSt/Publikationen/GrauePublikationen/GP_Germanys_dual_vocational_training_system.pdf. [42]

European Alliance for Apprenticeships (2021), *Examination and Certification in Luxembourg*, https://www.apprenticeship-toolbox.eu/standards-matching/examination-certification/91-examination-certification-in-luxembourg. [24]

European Alliance for Apprenticeships (2018), *Examination & Certification in Austria*, https://www.apprenticeship-toolbox.eu/standards-matching/examination-certification/88-examination-certification-in-austria. [34]

Eurydice (2020), *Assessment in Vocational Upper Secondary Education*, https://eacea.ec.europa.eu/national-policies/eurydice/content/assessment-vocational-upper-secondary-education-24_en. [20]

Field, S. (2021), *A World Without Maps: Assessment in Technical Education*, https://www.gatsby.org.uk/uploads/education/reports/pdf/assessment-in-technical-education-simon-field.pdf. [7]

Field, S. and A. Guez (2018), *Pathways of Progression: Between Technical and Vocational Education and Training and Post-Secondary Education.*, UNESCO, Paris, http://unesdoc.unesco.org/images/0026/002659/265943e.pdf. [8]

Finnish Ministry of Education and Culture (2017), *Reform of vocational upper secondary education*, https://minedu.fi/en/reform-of-vocational-upper-secondary-education. [5]

Government of Western Australia (2018), *Training Accreditation Council. Fact Sheet. Assuring the Quality of RTO: Processes, Practices and Products*, https://www.tac.wa.gov.au/SiteCollectionDocuments/D20%20006600.pdf (accessed on 24 January 2022). [37]

Haasler, S. (2020), "The German system of vocational education and training: challenges of gender, academisation and the integration of low-achieving youth", *Transfer: European Review of Labour and Research*, Vol. 26/1, pp. 57-71, http://dx.doi.org/10.1177/1024258919898115. [39]

IfATE (2021), *End-point assessment plan for Pipe Welder apprenticeship standard*, https://www.instituteforapprenticeships.org/media/3325/st0851_pipe_welder_l3_ap_final_for-publication_17072019.pdf. [9]

IfATE (2020), *External Quality Assurance Annual Report 2020*, https://www.instituteforapprenticeships.org/media/4724/eqa-annual-report.pdf. [38]

International Labour Organisation (2020), *ILO Toolkit for Quality Apprenticeships: Volume 2: Guide for Practitioners*, https://www.ilo.org/wcmsp5/groups/public/---ed_emp/---ifp_skills/documents/publication/wcms_751116.pdf. [15]

Karttunen, A. (2018), *The big VET reform in Finland*, https://nvl.org/content/the-big-vet-reform-in-finland. [6]

Kutsekoda Estonian Qualifications Authority (2021), *Estonian Qualifications Authority*, https://www.kutsekoda.ee/en/. [3]

Lee, M. and P. Newton (2021), *Systematic divergence between teacher and test-based assessment: literature review*, https://www.gov.uk/government/publications/systematic-divergence-between-teacher-and-test-based-assessment/systematic-divergence-between-teacher-and-test-based-assessment-literature-review#contents. [32]

Lerman, R. (2013), "Are employability skills learned in U.S. youth education and training programs?", *IZA J Labor Policy*, Vol. 2/6, https://doi.org/10.1186/2193-9004-2-6. [25]

Ministère de Solidarité et de Santé (2018), *Pour Les Étudiants Et Leurs Futurs Patients, Des Études Médicales Rénovées*, https://solidarites-sante.gouv.fr/IMG/pdf/180705_-_dp_-_etudes_medicales_renovees.pdf. [17]

National Electrotechnical Training (2021), *AM2*, https://www.netservices.org.uk/am2/. [14]

New Zealand Ministry of Education (2021), *Reliability and Validity*, https://assessment.tki.org.nz/Using-evidence-for-learning/Working-with-data/Concepts/Reliability-and-validity#:~:text=The%20reliability%20of%20an%20assessment,it%20was%20designed%20to%20measure. [10]

Norwegian Ministry of Education and Research (2006), *Education Act*, https://lovdata.no/dokument/SF/forskrift/2006-06-23-724/KAPITTEL_5-2#KAPITTEL_5-2. [30]

OECD (2018), *Getting Skills Right: Brazil*, Getting Skills Right, OECD Publishing, Paris, https://dx.doi.org/10.1787/9789264309838-en. [1]

Skills Development Scotland and Centre for Workbased Learning (2018), *Skills 4.0 A Skills Model to Drive Scotland's Future*, https://www.skillsdevelopmentscotland.co.uk/media/44684/skills-40_a-skills-model.pdf. [22]

Stanley, G. (2017), *Accreditation and Assessment in VET*, OUP. [18]

University of Exeter (2021), *Improving Formative Assessment in Vocational Education and Literacy, Language and Numeracy*, http://education.exeter.ac.uk/ifa/. [29]

Victoria State Government (2022), *Independent Assessment Portal*, https://independentassessment.vetassess.com.au/ (accessed on 2022 January 24). [33]

Yu, K. and G. Frempong (2012), "Standardise and individualise – an unsolvable tension in assessment?", *Education as Change*, pp. 143-157, http://dx.doi.org/10.1080/16823206.2012.692210. [19]

Annex 5.A. Defining occupational competence for a blacksmith in England: Knowledge, skills and behaviours required

Knowledge

- Health & Safety (H&S) - health & safety process, legislation and regulations in the forge and on site including COSHH, H&S at work act 1974. Knowledge of safe work processes that ensures the safety of self and others such as personal health surveillance, hazard recognition, risk assessment, method statements, disposal of waste, equipment inspection, personal protective equipment. Knowledge of exposure, risk and prevention of flash burns, arc eye, radiant heat, noise exposure and fumes as well as knowledge of preventing musculoskeletal and manual handling injuries.
- Materials - the properties and uses of materials used for blacksmithing such as the effects of heat and working on forgeable metals. The effects of combining metals and other media such as wood, stone or plastic. Modes of supply, methods for handling and storing resources. The effects of the environment and techniques for protecting metalwork.
- Tools - the key equipment, fixed and hand tools, the principles of operation, manufacture, set up, maintenance and safe use. Hand tools such as tongs, punches, chisels, hammers, anvil tools and jigs. Hand held machine tools such as drills and grinders. Fixed forge equipment such as power hammers, presses, forges, furnaces. Fixed fabrication equipment such as guillotines, rolls, metalworkers and linishers. Fixed welding equipment such as welding plant, profile cutters and extraction systems. Fixed machine equipment such as drills, lathes, milling and grinding machines.
- Quality - knowledge of quality standards including those expected by the client, employer, suppliers and regulatory bodies, including methods of recording work, use of product data sheets, International Standardisation Organisation (ISO) 9001, Conformete European (CE) marking and building regulations.
- Design – knowledge of elements and principles of design, drawing conventions and techniques by hand or computer aided design (CAD). Interpreting models and samples as part of the initial design process when presenting an idea to a client or as a component of design realisation when working out production samples.
- Manufacture, conservation and repair of metalwork - Finishing and protection methods and processes. The occupational roles and responsibilities within the processes regarding work relationships such as knowledge of those responsible for advising the client or other relevant parties, an appreciation of the costs of time and materials in the production of forged ironwork and the issues involved in seeking approval for work to commission or for direct retail.
- Setting up for work, problems that may occur and how to respond to them, knowledge of relevant mathematics and science such as volumes of metal required when calculating forging allowances, linear calculations for frameworks and bending, trigonometry for squaring and calculating angles when setting up working drawings or constructions, the chemistry and physics of ferrous metals in their heat treatment, the properties of common alloying elements and the chemistry of corrosion and its causes.
- Context of the craft - the context of the craft such as design styles, notable blacksmiths and artistic movements. Historical and contemporary processes and techniques.

Skills

- Health & Safety and working environment - maintain standards of health and safety for self and for others, using safe working practices. Prepare and maintain a safe working environment, where both hand and mechanical tools are used, as well as being able to safely handle fuel and light and operate the forge. Identify hazards and minimise risk in the working environment.
- Vocational interpretation and understanding - create and interpret specifications, samples, drawings, and other written and verbal instructions for the manufacture or repair of metalwork. The identification and appropriate response to problems such as calculating jointing, forging and bending allowances, creation of working templates or jigs from drawings, arriving at an appropriate order of dismantling and construction including testing and adjustment, seeking advice and guidance as appropriate.
- Design – produce vocational drawings, designs and models by hand or computer aided design (CAD) which can be interpreted by colleagues and clients when developing the final product.
- Manufacturing and repair processes - select and use the appropriate processes, techniques, materials, tools and equipment for manufacture or repair of metalwork and undertake the blacksmith making process to the industrial standard from inception to realisation. Plan and manage time effectively.
- Hot Forging - efficiently manage a forge or furnace when using forge tools to hot forge, form, cut and join metals by hand and machine.
- Thermal Welding and cutting - use hand operated thermal equipment, cutting and joining techniques to cut and join metals.
- Machining - use hand operated machine tools for cutting, drilling and shaping components.
- Bench work - use hand tools to cold cut and shape materials. Join materials using fastening systems.
- Tools, materials and equipment - carry out testing and adjustment. Manufacture, prepare and maintain materials, equipment and tools appropriately. Manufacture and maintain hand tools such as tongs, punches, chisels, hammers, anvil tools and jigs. Maintain equipment such as hand held machine tools, fixed forge equipment such as power hammers, presses, forges and furnaces. Fabrication, welding and engineering equipment. Preparing materials such as consumables, metal for the job, fixings and coatings.
- Finishing – clean, prepare and protect metalwork. Finish surfaces by specifying and applying specified surface treatments, coatings or coverings as required such as wire brushing, degreasing, descaling, polishing, waxing, oiling, painting and specifying sub-contract finishes such as hot dip galvanising, electro polishing and powder coating.
- Fitting - construct and fit work in the workshop and/or on site as appropriate, which includes assembly and dismantling of components and products and correcting faults in metalwork.

Behaviours

- Promote positive safety culture – ensure at all times that work is carried out in a safe way that does not put themselves or others at risk.
- Quality focused - work to appropriate quality standards such as working to client requirements, workshop samples, drawing specifications, historical listings, building regulations and workshop procedures, with efficient use of time, materials and resources. Record work and either self-evaluate or obtain feedback from others to improve work and working practice.

- Professionalism - have a strong professional work ethic including pride in work and attention to detail. Recognise the need for efficient and clear communication and the importance of working effectively with others. Promote and represent the craft, apply ethics and professional judgment in all areas of work. Take responsibility for own work and monitoring the work of others
- Self-development - keep up to date with best practice and emerging technologies within the sector. Obtain and offer constructive feedback to others, develop and maintain professional relationships.

Annex 5.B. Assessment in detail: Vocational assessment in Germany in apprenticeship - the example of plumber qualifications

Introduction: Apprenticeship in Germany

Roughly half of young people pursue apprenticeships in the dual system, a proportion that has been declining. In addition, for the some parts of the services sector there are programmes in vocational schools which are not apprenticeship.

The ability to change occupations and to switch between different school sites is limited and so the early allocation of pupils becomes a significant determinant of a candidate's later career (Haasler, 2020[39]). The system has been criticised for its lack of potential for social mobility and perpetuation of inequalities (Haasler, 2020[39]). Conversely apprenticeships enable smooth transition into work, resulting in low youth unemployment (2015: 7.2% of aged 15 to 24 versus 20.4% in the EU-28) (CEDEFOP, 2017[40])

Dual system (apprenticeship) takes the form of training with an approved employer (70% of the programme time) and theoretical education in a vocational school (30% of the time). In 2016, 68% of graduates remained employed by the firm in which they had trained (Haasler, 2020[39]). The period of training in the dual vocational education and training system is, for the majority of professions, 3 or 3.5 years long. A small number of diplomas are offered for a training period of 2 years, with the option of extending this training period to 3/3.5 years so as to acquire the complete set of skills required of the specific profession. The Vocational Training Act and Handicrafts Regulation Act (Handwerksordnung) provide the framework for shortening or lengthening of training periods, and allows for differences in trainees pre-traineeship skills and abilities.

For example, training for the "skilled worker for metal technology" lasts 2 years and provides for the basic knowledge required. If the trainee ends this training programme successfully, they can then extend the training by 1.5 years in order to acquire the skills and competencies necessary to be employed as a metal worker.

The company and the vocational school both have an educational responsibility and provide training across both theory and practice. In other words, the vocational school is not limited to teaching theory and the training within a company is not limited to practical work.

Pathways to further learning

At a tertiary level, vocationally qualified applicants without a school-based higher education entrance qualification can access advanced vocational training (AVT) leading to qualifications at EQF level 6, such as a technical engineer or industriemaster (Cedefop, 2017[41]). Exams for Industriemeister, for example, are organised uniformly across the country at the Chamber of Industry and Commerce (IHK). A prerequisite for attendance is a subject-specific vocational qualification and sufficient professional practice (regulated differently in the various specialist areas).

Employer engagement in certification and assessment

Apprenticeship certification requires 2 exams. The first takes the form of an intermediate examination or apprenticeship certification exam part I. The second, the final examination or apprenticeship certification exam part II, is taken towards the end of the training programme (at the end of the 3/3.5 years). Both examinations cover both theory and practice. The intermediate examination is used to provide both the candidate and the education company with an idea of their current performance in theory and in practice. Increasingly, the intermediate examination results are being used summatively in addition, and they contribute 30-40% of the overall score, with the final examination contributing the remainder.

There is a strict division between teaching and assessment in the dual system. Responsibility for assessing vocational skills lies with the public statutory bodies: the chambers of commerce and crafts. When final examinations are administered, teachers/trainers do not evaluate their own students (avoiding bias) and learning sites are not involved in the examination process (Euler, 2013[42]).

Examinations are administered by the Chambers (statutory employer organisations) and their appointed examining boards. Each board should comprise equal numbers of employers' and employee's representatives (at least two-thirds) and at least one vocational school teacher, all appointed by the competent body for a maximum period of five years (section 40, Vocational Training Act).

Quality assurance and oversight

The BIBB board provides recommendations for standardised model examination regulations in the vocational training act (BIBB, 2017, p. 41[43]).

The Vocational Training Act contains framework regulations for examinations (the details as to subject matter etc. are set forth by the relevant training regulations and ordinances on further training).

The chamber develops examination regulations subject to the approval of the federal government. The regulations cover: admission, structure, evaluation procedures, certification, breaches of the regulations and resits (BIBB, 2017[43]).

Quality Assurance of the examinations is based on impartiality and objectivity. This is based on regulations for the examiners, i.e. that the trainers are not involved in the assessment themselves. Also, that individual examination performances are evaluated by at least two examiners.

Accelerated and alternative entry routes to the final apprenticeship examination

- Trainees can be admitted in advance (before the end of the training period) if their performance justifies it.
- Individuals who have worked in a specific profession for a duration of 1.5 times the duration of the training period for said profession, or who can provide certifications demonstrating that they possess the equivalent and necessary skills and competencies, can also be admitted.

Grading and certification

The examinations are graded as follows:

- 100-92 points = 1 = excellent
- 91 - 81 points = 2 = good
- 80 - 67 points = 3 = average

- 66 - 50 points = 4 = pass
- 49 - 30 points = 5 = poor
- 29 - 0 points = 6 = fail.

If a candidate does not pass the examination, they can resit the assessment up to two times.

In 2016, 444 200 final exams (413 200 initial exams, 31 000 repeat exams) were held and 399 800 people completed their vocational training by passing a final examination. 91.9 % of participants (370 600 people) succeeded in doing so at their first attempt.

Certification

The apprentices receive three different certificates (Appreniceship toolbox, 2019[44]):
- the examination certificate (*Facharbeiterbrief/Gesellenbrief*) provided by the chamber
- the leaving certificate of the vocational school and
- the reference of the training company.

A competent body, i.e. Chamber of Industry and Commerce (IHK) or the Chamber of Skilled Crafts and Small Businesses (HWK), issues the certificate. They organise the entire exam details (dates, exam committees) in the 'Länder' (federal states) and issue the exam certificates and final certificates (Bliem, Petanovitsch and Schmid, 2016, p. 34[45]).

Trainees can request that the result of their vocational school achievements will be listed on the chamber certificate. They can also request that their certificate be accompanied by a translation in English and/or French so as to promote mobility (BIBB, 2017[46]).

In-company trainers also issue a certificate to their apprentices at the end of the training relationship, indicating the nature, duration and objective of the vocational training and the vocational skills, knowledge and abilities acquired by the apprentice (BIBB, 2017[46]).

Example: Plumber

Taken from the Ordinance on Vocational Training for Plumbers and Plumbing Technicians (Klempner), From 21 June 2013 (BIBB, 2016[47]).

The journeyman's examination consists of the two parts 1 and 2.

Part 1 of the journeyman's examination ('work order' – 30% of marks)

Part 1 of the journeyman's examination shall take place before the end of the of the second year of training. the examinee should be able to:

a) use technical documentation, plan working steps measurements and to record them, to plan materials and tools
b) process material manually and mechanically, form, join and assemble material, produce templates and mould parts
c) take measures for work organisation, safety and health protection at work, environmental protection and quality assurance
d) to show the technical background relevant to the examination task
e) to show the technical background relevant to the examination task and to justify the procedure.

The examinee is to carry out a **work task typical of the occupation (duration: 7 hours)**, to conduct a situational technical discussion (duration: 15 minutes) relating to it and complete tasks in writing (60 minutes) which relate to the content of the work task.

Part 2 of the examination

Part 2 of the journeyman's examination involves three components: 'customer order'; 'production, assembly and maintenance technology' and 'economic and social studies'.

1. **customer order (40% of the marks).**

The following requirements apply to the customer order examination area:

a) The examinee is to prove that he is able to work processes and sub-tasks taking into account economic, technical, organisational and time specifications
b) Process, manufacture and assemble components or subassemblies, test them for function and fit them
c) Check the results of work for accuracy of fit, secure and visual impression and to carry out corrective measures
d) Hand over components or assemblies to the customer, provide technical information, instruct customers and prepare acceptance reports
e) Explain the technical background relevant to the customer's order and to justify the procedure.

Areas that can be selected:

a) roof cladding;
b) façade cladding;
c) drainage systems for precipitation water;
d) moulded parts of ventilation technology.

The candidate is to produce a test piece (16 hours), document the production with documents customary in practice and conduct an order-related technical discussion (20 minutes max duration). The examination time is 16 hours.

2. **Assembly and maintenance technology (20% of the marks).**

The examinee is to prove that he is able to:

a) draw up working plans for customer orders and developments
b) describe the procedure for the manufacture of a component or an assembly of plumbing technology plumbing technology
c) identify faults, describe causes, assess the consequences and describe measures to eliminate them
d) to deal with technical problems with linked information technology, technological and mathematical facts
e) describe measures for preventive maintenance measures
f) take into account safety, economic efficiency and environmental protection into account.

The candidate shall complete a written assessment for the practical task. The examination time shall be 240 minutes.

3. **Economics and social studies (10% of the marks).**

In a written examination (60 minutes) in an occupation-related task, the candidate shall prove that they are able to present and assess general, economic and social contexts of the world of work and professions.

Passing regulations

The journeyman's examination is passed if:

a) The overall result of Part 1 and Part 2 is "sufficient"
b) The score for "customer orders" is "sufficient"
c) The result of Part 2 is "sufficient"
d) At least one further examination area of Part 2 is "sufficient"
e) No examination area of Part 2 can be "unsatisfactory".